D1093705

The Griffith Actresses

Also by Anthony Slide

Early American Cinema

The Griffith Actresses

by

Anthony Slide

South Brunswick and New York:
A. S. Barnes and Company
London: The Tantivy Press

A. S. Barnes and Co., Inc.
Cranbury, New Jersey 08512

The Tantivy Press
108 New Bond St.
London W1Y OQX, England

Library of Congress Cataloging in Publication Data
Slide, Anthony.
    The Griffith actresses.
    Bibliography: p.
    1. Griffith, David Wark, 1875–1948.
2. Moving-picture actors and actresses—United States—Biography. I. Title.
PN1998.A3G78   791.43′0233′0924   72-6373
ISBN 0-498-01018-X

SBN: 90073071 4 (U.K.)
PRINTED IN THE UNITED STATES OF AMERICA

For
Blanche Sweet

And we may believe they walk again,
as they did long years ago.
    —Final title in *True Heart Susie*

Contents

Acknowledgments

In the preparation of this book I have become indebted to many people. In New York, I wish to thank William K. Everson and Eileen Bowser for arranging screenings for me, and also in the latter's case for allowing me the use of the research facilities of the Museum of Modern Art. In Rochester, both James Card and George Pratt of George Eastman House offered me every kindness, and I must also thank George Pratt for his hospitality on my two visits to Rochester. In London, I wish to thank Bert Langdon and John Cunningham for screening films from their collections for me, and also Harold Dunham, Philip Kendall and the staff of the National Film Archive. I must also thank Bill Doyle, T. A. Johnson, and especially Edward Wagenknecht, whose help and encouragement I much appreciate.

Finally, I wish to thank the following for talking to me about themselves and their contemporaries:

Miss Lillian Gish
Miss Anita Loos
Miss Bessie Love
Mr. Jack Mulhall
Mr. Charles "Buddy" Rogers
Mr. Charles Rosher
Miss Blanche Sweet
Mr. Herbert Wilcox

Unless otherwise indicated, all quotations from the aforementioned were taken during interviews with the author. Internal footnotes refer to the numbered bibliography at the end of this volume.

The Griffith Actresses

1

What Made a Griffith Girl?

David Wark Griffith was born in Crestwood, Kentucky, on January 22, 1875; he was the fourth son of Jacob Wark Griffith, a one-time Confederate colonel. In 1908 he joined the American Biograph Company as an actor, after having been previously employed in the same capacity by the Edison Company. On July 14, 1908, his first film as a director, *The Adventures of Dollie,* was released. His last production, *The Struggle,* was released on December 10, 1931. He died in Hollywood on July 23, 1948.

That, in one cold precise paragraph, sums up the career of D. W. Griffith, the man who not only invented screen syntax, but also—and more importantly—gave the cinema the most precious gift of all, beauty. That beauty he presented to film audiences to a large extent through the actresses whom he used in his productions, actresses who studied individually might appear to have little in common but who together had one major common denominator: they were all Griffith Girls.

What made a Griffith girl? Physically, they were all small, slim, and young, the last attribute perhaps being the most important. "We pick the little women because the world loves youth, and all its wistful sweetness. . . . Youth with its dreams and sweetness, youth with its romance and adventure! For in the theater, as in our families, we look to youth for beauty and often for example. We sit in the twilight

David Wark Griffith: The Creator

of the theater and in terms of youth, upon faces enlarged, we see thoughts that are personal to us, with the privilege of supplying our own words and messages as they may fit our individual experiences in life."

All the Griffith girls (excluding, of course, the character actresses) were less than twenty years of age when they came under his direction; Blanche Sweet was not yet fourteen when she joined Biograph, and Carol Dempster was eighteen when she made *True Heart Susie,* as was Miriam Cooper when she made *Intolerance.*

It is often said, foolishly, that the Griffith heroine was always ethereal. Which other Griffith actress, aside from Lillian Gish, can be described as ethereal? Certainly not Blanche Sweet or Mae Marsh or Clarine Seymour. As "The Little Disturber" in *Hearts of the World,* Dorothy Gish was anything but ethereal, and Carol Dempster was only ethereal in as much as she was trying to emulate Lillian Gish. If anything a Griffith heroine had many masculine traits, in that she would fight for what she desired, and if she did not get it, it was not through want of trying.

The quality which made these actresses so special, the quality which Griffith saw in each of them—perhaps not instantly, but very soon after the first meeting—was, I believe, "soul." By "soul" I mean emotion, an inner quality that could be brought to the surface and exposed before the camera: an inner quality that might remain dormant until its possessor came into contact with a mesmerist, a Svengali, a D. W. Griffith.

"Soul" was an expression Griffith often referred to when discussing film acting: "The actor with the Soul enters into the work with all the ardor there is in him. He feels his part, he is living his part, and the result is a good picture. . . . For principals I must have people with souls, people who know and feel their parts, and who express every single feeling in the entire gamut of emotions with their muscles. . . . It isn't what you do with your face or your hands, it's the light within. If you have that light, it doesn't matter just what you do before the camera."

Griffith's choice of actresses seldom faltered. He always seemed to know who had that "light within," although it wasn't always apparent the first time he worked with a particular actress. Linda Arvidson comments, regarding Blanche Sweet, that when she first applied for work at American Biograph, he was "as yet unwilling to grant that she had any soul or feeling in her work." Occasionally he failed to spot that light at all, as with Florence Lawrence, whom he allowed without demur to leave American Biograph and join Carl Laemmle.

All these players remained loyal to Griffith; their devotion was absolute. Lillian Gish has shown her devotion not only in the title of her autobiography, but in one of her acknowledgements therein: "To D. W. Griffith who taught me it was more fun to work than to play." (24) Lionel Barrymore wrote, "Bless him, he always tried to make one feel his contribution was great even though it might have been piffle." (40) All of his players have protected his good name throughout the years. It is almost impossible to find anyone who has ever worked for Griffith who has one word of criticism of him. (One almost feels obligated to use a capital "H" for his or him.) The general feeling about the man by all who knew him was summed up by Blanche Sweet, when we discussed his funeral.

"I did go to his funeral, although I don't believe in funerals. But I did go there, and felt very badly about it, because there were quite a lot of people there, but on the other hand, all of Hollywood should have been there—standing. All of Hollywood, because without him, maybe someone else would have come along and done it, maybe, but maybe not. Anyway, he did it. And he contributed more, actually, to making motion pictures than anybody else. There have been a lot of people, men and women, who had done a great deal for films, contributed a lot, but nobody did quite as much as he did. And I really felt that everybody who ever worked in the films should have been there. Well, that's one reason why I don't believe in funerals."

This volume chronicles lives and careers of several of the Griffith girls. Without him most, maybe all, would be unknown today, but I also like to think that his success owed much to their presence in his films. He brought out the best in them, and they responded by assuring his films—through their acting—a place in the history of the cinema.

In 1928, D. W. Griffith addressed the Academy of Motion Picture Arts and Sciences with the following words: "When motion pictures have created something to compare with the plays of Euripides, that have lasted two thousand years, or the works of Homer, or the plays of Shakespeare, or Ibsen, or Keats's 'Ode to a Nightingale,' the music of Handel, Bach, and Wagner, then let us call our form of entertainment an art, but not before." Griffith was not a modest man; I believe he knew when he made that speech that his films had equalled the works of Homer, Shakespeare, or Handel, that *Broken Blossoms* was comparable in beauty to "Ode to a Nightingale." But, as in any great man's work, it was the collaborators, the interpreters, who played their part as well. The Griffith girls were the Sarah Bernhardt and the Julia Marlowe to his Shakespeare, the Kirsten Flagsted to his Wagner. To them also should be given the praise and the glory. We shall not see David Wark Griffith's like again; nor, I fear, shall we see theirs—the Griffith Girls'.

2

The Ladies of the Biograph

The children who tripped to fortune
up the steps of 11 East 14th Street.
—Iris Barry (3)

The studios of the American Biograph Company at 11 East 14th
Street were the finest training ground any silent film actress (or actor
for that matter) could desire. It is doubtful that any other of the
early companies, with the possible exception of Vitagraph, produced
so many embryo stars. Mary Pickford, Blanche Sweet, Mae Marsh,
Mabel Normand, Lillian and Dorothy Gish were all stars who served
their apprenticeship with the American Biograph Company.

But there were also many fine actresses working at the studios
who never became stars, but whose presence in films, usually in character roles, was something that was received with a sigh of appreciation and thanks. Kate Bruce, Florence Lawrence, Josephine Crowell,
Marion Leonard, Claire McDowell, and Linda Arvidson were
actresses whose faces, if not names, were known and loved by filmgoers during the teens and twenties. They have all long since passed
on, but the memory of their performances remains undimmed for all

17

The studios of the American Biograph Company at 11 East 14th Street, New York

those who loved the silent cinema, and to them this chapter is dedicated.

The character actress whose name immediately springs to mind when one thinks of the D. W. Griffith stock company is Kate Bruce.

Mabel Normand. Linda Arvidson wrote, she was "the most wonderful girl in the world, the most beautiful and the best sport. Daring, reckless, and generous-hearted to a fault, she was like a frisky young colt that would brook no bridle."

"Fortunate Brucie," as Linda Arvidson wrote, "she seems never to have had to hunt a job since that long ago day when D. W. Griffith picked her as a member of the old Biograph Stock Company. Little bits or big parts mattered nothing to 'Brucie' as long as she was working with us." (1) Blanche Sweet recalled her as "a dear person, very quiet, very calm. Rather shy, she never had much to say. She played a great many of the mothers, of course, always the sweeter, gentle characters—she was that."

Kate Bruce seems to have been everyone's mother; in *Hearts of*

Kate Bruce

Kate Bruce with Richard Barthelmess in a posed portrait for *Way Down East*

the World she is aptly described as "the fussy little mother." Apart from her maternal roles in Griffith productions, she was the mother of Thomas Meighan (*City of Silent Men*, 1921), Richard Barthelmess (*Experience*, 1921), Lloyd Hamilton (*His Darker Self*, 1924), Milton Sills (*I Want My Man*, 1925), Gladys Hulette (*A Bowery*

Cinderella, 1927), John Bowers (*Ragtime,* 1927), and Olive Borden (*The Secret Studio,* 1927). She even appeared, albeit briefly, as a mother in Thomas Ince's production of *Civilization* (1916) and for a few seconds lightened a rather gloomy picture. But there was also a darker side to her characterizations. She could play a sly old lady, as she did in *True Heart Susie,* in which, just before Harron proposes to Clarine Seymour, Kate digs her in the ribs and whispers "Now's your chance."

Nothing seems to be known about Kate Bruce's background, where she was born, or how she first came to the Biograph. She died on April 2, 1946 at the age of 88. In the last years of Brucie's life, she had been supported by Lillian Gish. She was, it appears, already at American Biograph when Griffith first began directing, but she did not leave the company in 1913 to go with him to Reliance-Majestic, for her next appearance in a Griffith production after his Biograph period was in *Intolerance* (1916). Kate appeared in most of Griffith's productions from then onwards until *The White Rose* in 1924. Then came a break, but she was back with him again for his last production, *The Struggle,* with an uncredited appearance. During what is to prove a catastrophic party, there is a ring on the doorbell, and who should be standing there but Kate Bruce (at her appearance I nearly fell out of my seat with excitement while watching the film at the Museum of Modern Art). We don't hear her voice, but she is led to a chair in the corner of the room, where she sits, partly obscured by a door, sipping an unidentified nonalcoholic beverage. So Griffith said his final screen farewell to a great old lady.

If Kate Bruce represents sweetness to all Griffith devotees, it is Josephine Crowell who represents evil; a 1921 article about her described her as "The Wickedest Woman in Pictures." I cannot read about Catherine de Medici without seeing Josephine Crowell's face as she plots the massacre of the Huguenots in *Intolerance.* But just as it is wrong to label Kate Bruce "a sweet old lady," it is equally wrong to tie a label on Josephine Crowell. She was the kindly Mrs. Cameron in *The Birth of a Nation,* the mother of John Howard Payne in *Home Sweet Home,* Lillian Gish's mother in *Hearts of the World,* and Aunt Gladys, "an old fusspot" who cares for Mary Pickford's Unity Blake in *Stella Maris.* And sometimes, as in *Rebecca of Sunnybrook Farm,* she put on a hard face to hide a kind heart; we knew just how much she really loved Mary Pickford, despite the hardness of her reply to Mary's gift of flowers at her sickbed: "I ain't dead yet, don't mess up the bed with yer flowers."

Josephine Bonaparte Crowell was born in Halifax, Canada, of

"We must destroy or be destroyed." Josephine Crowell in *Intolerance*

Josephine Crowell with John Gilbert and Roy D'Arcy in Erich von Stroheim's
The Merry Widow (1925)

French Canadian parents, and came to films after an extensive stage career in which she usually played comedy roles. (The nearest she ever came to playing comedy on the screen was in Victor Fleming's 1926 *Mantrap,* in which she appeared as the old gossip, disapproving of Clara Bow.) She definitely first worked for Griffith at American Biograph, and may be glimpsed as one of the parents in *The School Teacher and the Waif* (released June 27, 1912). Of how she came to portray Catherine de Medici in *Intolerance,* she explained: "It was just fate that made me so wicked on the screen—fate and David Griffith. When he was rehearsing another player for the part of Catherine de Medici I happened to be on the set, and he asked me to run through a scene. For some reason he liked my work in that type, and he transferred the part to me. I was ashamed of myself when I saw the previews. I looked so bad I was afraid of myself. Since then, whenever he had a particularly awful part, he made me do it, and other directors have the habit of calling me up at all hours of the day and night and asking me if I can come out and poison a little blond child in the morning!" (19) She more than surpassed her wickedness in *Intolerance* with her performance in *The Greatest Question,* in which she brutally whipped Lillian Gish and then, brandishing a gun, chased her around the house, aptly described as "the citadel of the evil legions."

Josephine Crowell, of course, made many appearances in non-Griffith films, including, apart from those already mentioned, Erich von Stroheim's *The Merry Widow* (1925), Marshall Neilan's *The Sporting Venus* (1925), Paul Leni's *The Man Who Laughs* (1927), and Cecil B. DeMille's *King of Kings* (1927). The brown-haired, kindly-faced lady, who always longed to play screen comedy, died in Amityville, Long Island, on July 27, 1932.

The original Biograph Girl, indeed the actress who might rightly be described as the world's first film star, was Florence Lawrence. (American Biograph, like its contemporary companies, did not publish the names of its players, and so the Biograph leading lady came to be known as the Biograph Girl, just as the leading actress with the Vitagraph Company, Florence Turner, was known as the Vitagraph Girl. Gradually all the companies except American Biograph came around to naming their players. American Biograph steadfastly refused to divulge its players' identities, despite repeated requests from filmgoers. Eventually, the British distributors of Biograph productions were forced to give fictitious names to the players, and a record of such names is given in Appendix One.)

During her years with Griffith at American Biograph, Miss Lawrence had a tremendous following among both the filmgoers and the critics. She played opposite John Compson in a series of eleven Jones family comedies: *The Smoked Husband* (released September 25, 1908), *Mr. Jones at he Ball, Mr. Jones Entertains, Mr. Jones Has a Card Party, Jones and the Lady Book Agent, The Jones* [sic] *Have Amateur Theatricals, Jones and His New Neighbors, Her First Biscuits, The Peach Basket Hat, Mr. Jones's Lover* and *Mr. Jones and the Burglar* (released August 9, 1909). The following synopsis of *The Jones Have Amateur Theatricals* (released February 18, 1909) gives a general idea of the type of humor that was popular in 1909. Mrs. Jones receives a note that the Amateur Dramatic Club is to hold its next meeting at her home. The players arrive, and Mr. Jones is selected to play the lover to Mrs. Trouble. Mrs. Jones misunderstands the attention Jones is paying Mrs. Trouble, and attacks him. When all is explained to her, she elects to play the woman's role; an actor is chosen to play her lover, and it is then Mr. Jones's turn to misunderstand the situation. He and some fellow actors have been drinking, and the Club meeting breaks up in confusion. The film ends, as it had begun, with the Joneses sitting in their respective armchairs, yawning. *The Moving Picture World* (February 27, 1909) described it as "good, clean comedy."

Miss Lawrence did not confine herself to slapstick comedy; she played the title role in *Lady Helen's Escapade,* released on April 19, 1909, which *Moving Picture World* thought "a delightfully refined comedy of manners." The magazine continued, "Of course, the chief honors of the picture are borne by the now famous Biograph Girl, who must be gratified by the silent celebrity she has achieved. This lady combines with very great personal attractions very fine dramatic ability indeed."

Of her excellent dramatic performance opposite Arthur Johnson in *Resurrection,* released May 20, 1909, *The Moving Picture World* had this to say: "Then the acting of the leading woman and the prince—how fine and tragic the former is! How excellent the latter! We do not know the lady's name, but certainly she seems to us to have a very fine command of her emotions and to be able to express these emotions before such an unemotional thing as a camera. A very ordinary person indeed can act before a crowded house of interested men and women, but it takes a genius to do so with real feeling on a moving picture stage. For there is no eager, sympathetic audience of thousands before you there, but only the staff of the company or the matter-of-fact person who turns the handle and exposes so many feet of sensitized celluloid per minute on the players."

The Moving Picture World of June 5, 1909 announced that Carl Laemmle was to become a "film manufacturer," and the issue of October 23 of the same year announced the first release of the Imp Company. Late in 1909, Miss Lawrence left Griffith and the Biograph Company, and joined Carl Laemmle—the Biograph Girl was now the Imp Girl. A new actress, Mary Pickford, became the Biograph Girl, but the public was not fooled. A Mr. P. C. Lever of Coos Bay, Oregon, wrote to *The Moving Picture World* (February 19, 1910):

> The Biograph Girl who won all the hearts, male and female, in this neck of the woods was the one who used to play Mrs. Jones in the Jones comedies. I could mention a lot more of her parts, but that one is the easiest to clearly and briefly designate. She has been gone from the 'bunch' for months and the Biograph people ought to be lynched for letting her get away. She is, or was, with the Imp, and appeared in *The Forest Ranger's Daughter,* which dropped in here on a special occasion. Look in the Imp ad. in your issue and you will see a horribly poor picture of her. Now that is, or was, the Biograph Girl—and I am confident that you could find about 8,000,000 people in the United States who would agree with me. You could find a lot of them in this town.
>
> But that girl was simply out of sight—unapproachable. She was in a class by herself. In every part she played she was an exquisite delight. Whether comic, pathetic, dramatic, tragic, or any other old thing, she simply took the rag right off. The power of expression that lay in her features was nothing less than marvelous, and the lightning changes were a wonder. In fact, she was a wonder altogether, and her versatility would be unbelievable if a fellow hadn't seen it. To see her play Mrs. Jones in a tantrum and then see her as the Russian Nihilist girl, for instance, in a drama of which I have forgotten the name; as a young girl; as a mother; to see her as a highly polished society lady one time, and at another time see her straddle a cayuse as a Western girl and ride like a wild Indian—to see her take these widely varying parts and play each as though she were in her native element, with every pose and motion and expression in perfect harmony with the character—all this was a revelation. And to see her in a love scene was enough to draw a fellow right across the continent, if he were not fifty years old and married—and broke.
>
> And now you think someone else is the Biograph Girl! If you think I am off my base, you go and see the girl in some Imp picture where she has a chance—if they make any such. And that is the deuce of it. She doesn't belong anywhere else but with Biograph people. They are the only ones who seem to have regularly plays that call for and bring out her grade of talent.

Sadly, Florence Lawrence's transfer to the Imp Company was to mark the beginning of the end for her career. She became the forgotten star. In 1933 she joined MGM's stock company of ex-silent stars, who were kept on the regular payroll and given occasional "walk-ons." On December 28, 1938, she took her own life.

The "grand lady" of the Biograph Company was undoubtedly Marion Leonard. She is probably best remembered for her performance in *The Lonely Villa*, in which she portrayed the mother

Florence Lawrence

of Adele de Garde and Mary Pickford, who is terrorised by burglars while her husband is decoyed away. The critic of *The Moving Picture World* was quite carried away by the film: "The Biograph heroine is as handsome and graceful as ever. We really felt inclined to kick that burglar man for so unceremoniously stripping the jewels from this fair lady's neck."

Marion Leonard's stay with American Biograph was not lengthy. She returned to the stage in late 1909 or early 1910, and when she reappeared in films in October, 1910, it was as leading lady with the Carlton Stock Company (producers of Reliance Films). Her first release for that company was *In the Gray of the Dawn,* which also featured Arthur Johnson, Henry B. Walthall, James Kirkwood, Frances Burns, Gertrude Robinson, and Phillips Smalley: a very im-

Grace Henderson: A portrait issued for her admirers in England, and thus signed "Margaret Winter"

pressive array of talent indeed. In 1913, Monopol starred her in a series of three-reelers, including *Those Who Live in Glass Houses*, in which "love, hatred, romance, repentance and a true Christian spirit were beautifully blended into a story of gripping heart interest." For the same company, she also made *The Seed of the Fathers*, a six-reeler directed and scripted by S. E. V. Taylor, to whom Miss Leonard was married, and whose name will, of course, always be associated with D. W. Griffith.

The Taylors were two of the first residents of the Motion Picture Country House in Woodland Hills, California, and it was there that Marion Leonard died on January 9, 1956, at the age of seventy-four.

According to Linda Arvidson, however, at the Biograph studio "our *grande dame* of quality" was Grace Henderson (1). Certainly from her performances I would agree with Linda Arvidson's use of the word "quality" to describe her, but Grace Henderson always looked too pleasant and simply "nice" to be a "grande dame." Blanche Sweet remembered Mrs. Henderson with particular affection. "There was one magnificent woman; she was an elder woman—quite a guide in my life—and nothing very much has ever been said about her, and her name was Grace Henderson. She came from the theatre, and she had been a beauty. She was called what at that time had been termed the toast of Paris—and she had been the toast of Paris, and of this country, and, I daresay, England. She had known and, I believe, played with Maurice Barrymore. She was a cultured woman, still very beautiful, Oh, the loveliest skin you've ever seen. Well-groomed, well-mannered, and she became quite an influence in my life, in my reading, in my viewpoint, and I think that she was interested in me as a person. She could see that I was very young and didn't know very much. I remember her with great, great regard."

As far as I can ascertain, Mrs. Henderson returned to the stage after serving her time with the Biograph Company; she died in New York on October 30, 1944.

Another actress whom Blanche Sweet also remembered with affection was Claire McDowell, the wife of Biograph actor Charles Hill Mailes (who died in 1937). Claire was born and educated in New York City, and had had an extensive stage career under the management of Charles Frohman, William Brady, and others before beginning a six year sojourn with American Biograph. It is an unexplained mystery why Griffith did not ask her to go with him to Reliance-Majestic. Instead she went to Universal and then Triangle. She played minor character roles in films well into the sound era, and it is interesting that the first of such roles was in Mary Pickford's *The*

Heart o' the Hills (1919), since she had played opposite Mary in Biograph's *The Female of the Species* (released April 15, 1912). She died in Hollywood on October 24, 1966.

It is perhaps appropriate that this chapter should end with Linda Arvidson, to whom we should be eternally grateful for her fine—albeit sometimes inaccurate—volume of reminiscences of those days, *When the Movies Were Young*. Born in San Francisco in 1884, Linda Johnson had been a child actress with the Alcazar Stock Company. As Mrs. D. W. Griffith she was the great man's companion through the most trying period of his life when he was working as an actor in companies which cannot even be described as second-rate. She was also with him on what was to be, although he probably did not realise it at the time, the most momentous day of his life—the first public screening, at Keith and Proctor's Union Square Theatre, of his first directorial work, *The Adventures of Dollie*. This is all covered in her valuable book.

After parting from Griffith, she joined the American Kinemacolor Company, whose studios were at 4500 Sunset Boulevard, where she

Claire McDowell (center) with Mary Pickford and Dorothy Bernard in *The Female of the Species* (frame enlargement)

appeared in, among other films, *The Scarlet Letter*. Of her performance the English magazine *The Bioscope* wrote, "A most delicate and deeply pathetic study is given by an actress who is as beautiful as she is clever." Linda Arvidson's later life, as seen from the present, seems fairly sordid. She spent much of her time and money in employing private detectives to "shadow" Griffith, in order that she might blackmail him. In a newspaper report of February 16, 1937, Griffith said, "She charged me with having illicit relations with other women and, until she was prevented, interfered with my direction of motion pictures, assumed the direction herself, and falsely asserted she was the author of stories I had written. Otherwise, she threatened and persecuted me to such an extent it became impossible for me to live with her."

This poor, unhappy woman died in New York on July 26, 1949, almost a year to the day after Griffith's passing. There can be no Biograph actress who would not echo the sentiments she expressed in *When the Movies Were Young*: "I, for one, am glad I served my novitiate in a day when we could afford to be good fellows, and our hearts were young enough and happy enough to enjoy the gypsying way of life."

3

Blanche Sweet

One of the greatest actresses of all time.
—Herbert Wilcox

Some years ago, I was lunching in Dublin with Irish actor Michael
MacLiammoir, producer Hilton Edwards, and film historian Liam
O'Leary. The conversation soon got around to silent films in general
and D. W. Griffith in particular, and naturally the name Lillian Gish
came up. MacLiammoir began recalling the silent films of Lillian that
he had seen as a young man. Suddenly he stopped, and said, "But do
you recall a marvelous film, *Judith of Bethulia,* and that great actress
Blanche Sweet?" And then he began recounting incidents in a film
he had not seen in fifty years.

I must confess I was surprised that after so many years of absence
from the screen, Blanche Sweet should be so well remembered by
MacLiammoir. For expressing such surprise I must now confess my
shame, for I now know that to all those who grew up with the silent
cinema, Blanche Sweet represented dramatic acting at its finest. And
she should be remembered, because she was a great, great actress.

As to how much of her acting ability was of her own making and
how much of it stems from her schooling with D. W. Griffith it is
difficult to say. Linda Arvidson wrote that Griffith "hardly expected
her to set the world afire," and that he was at first "unwilling to grant

Blanche Sweet: An early portrait

that she had any soul or feeling in her work." Undoubtedly, she gave some brilliant performances in the Biograph and Mutual pictures she made for Griffith, particularly in *The Painted Lady* and *Judith of*

Bethulia, both of which I shall discuss later, but she also proved that in her post-Griffith career, with not always the most helpful or intelligent of directors, she could more than equal her acting in those early dramatic roles. Her appalling performances in some Biograph one-reelers—I'm thinking particularly of *The Battle*—make me feel that her acting did not depend on Griffith's direction, or on anyone else's for that matter, but on her and her alone.

Sarah Blanche Sweet was born in Chicago on June 18, 1896; contrary to what many people believe, Sweet was her real name. She was brought up by her grandmother, Cora Blanche Alexander, to whom Blanche was devoted. It was Mrs. Alexander who introduced the young Blanche to the stage and, as Blanche recalls, "I had done a vaudeville sketch, which I've since learned was something from Dickens, and I loved it." Blanche was also taking dancing lessons from Ruth St. Denis, lessons she was to put to good use later with Gertrude Hoffman.

Even in childhood, a mixture of pride and stubbornness, traits which were to be much in evidence during her film career, was apparent. "I was about four years old, I guess. My grandmother and I were in Cincinnati and Richard Mansfield was going to play there. As was the custom if the part was not large, if there were any children needed, they would get them from city to city. They have children, and pick from them—so I was picked, and I wouldn't do it. And my grandmother and I—I don't know if I knew it or not, it may be so—we both needed money to eat. And I wouldn't play that part. I can remember my grandmother taking me around the backdrop, pleading with me to play the part—she should have hit me. And I said 'No. I don't like his face.'" Some years later, Harry Carr was to sum up her personality in an article in *Motion Picture Magazine*: "Blanche has a fierce, unconquerable heart and a tender, sensitive soul. It's a terrible mixture . . . a sensitive, brooding soul with thoughts and impressions so sensitized and an emotion so deep that she dares not bare it to the world—nor to herself." (13)

In 1909, shortage of money persuaded Blanche and her grandmother to investigate films, and a friend suggested they try the Biograph Company. "So my grandmother and I went down, and in the outer foyer, which has been so much described, we made inquiries at a window, and they gave us a form, and we filled that out, and heard nothing. So that was the Biograph Company! Then we made our way up to the Edison Company, which was way uptown, and we had better luck there. They put me into a film the next day as an extra. All I remember about it was that it was raining, and I was under an umbrella. I don't remember who directed it; I don't remember who was in it; I don't remember anything about it, except it was Edison. And then they gave me a picture after that—*A Man with Three Wives.*"

This film was copyrighted by the Edison Company on November 12, 1909. A comedy 440 feet in length, it concerned Jack Howard and his friend Ralph, who shared an artists' studio in Greenwich Village. Jack had married against the wishes of his wealthy Uncle Peter, and the only way he could safeguard his interest in his uncle's fortune was to pass off his wife as that of the already-married Ralph. Jack's mother-in-law arrives on the scene, is horrified to discover a model in the studio, but mollified when Jack introduces her as Ralph's wife. The film ends, seven minutes after it had begun, with Jack's wife charming the uncle, who is attracted to the model, and the entire company dance around the irate mother-in-law. Blanche played one of the "wives," but which one she does not recall, and unhappily neither the film itself nor any stills from it are known to have survived.

After this one featured role at Edison, Blanche, with her grandmother, decided to try the Biograph Company again. "The same person who said go down to Biograph said 'Did you see Griffith?' and we said 'No, we just saw a window and a form.' 'Well, go down and see Griffith.' So we did. We asked for Griffith, and he eventually came out and talked to me. And he said 'Well, you can be in a film this afternoon.' "

And so Blanche Sweet made her first screen appearance with Biograph as an extra in *A Corner in Wheat,* released on December 13, 1909. Based on two works by Frank Norris, a novel *The Octopus* and a short story "A Deal in Wheat," the film featured Biograph regulars Henry B. Walthall, James Kirkwood, Mack Sennett, and Kate Bruce.

Blanche was not particularly impressed with Griffith at the beginning. "He was just somebody who was directing a film. I guess it took me a good year or more to realise I was working with a very unusual man, a very understanding person, a person who knew a great deal about people and things and acting. I guess I was slow. On the other hand—I've thought about this—it could also be that his personality was growing. Maybe he wasn't the great man in the beginning, and maybe he was developing along with the films that he was developing. Probably that was it; nobody will ever know which it was."

In the three years that she worked with American Biograph, Blanche was to become the company's most important player. She appeared in over seventy of the company's releases, in most cases

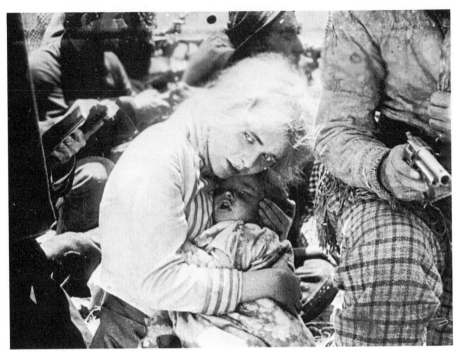

Blanche Sweet in *The Massacre* (frame enlargement)

Blanche Sweet with Charles Mailes in *Oil and Water* (frame enlargement)

Blanche Sweet with Walter Miller, Henry B. Walthall and unidentified actress in *Oil and Water* (frame enlargement)

Blanche Sweet in *The Painted Lady* (frame enlargement)

Judith of Bethulia: Judith (Blanche Sweet) with her maid (Kate Bruce)

playing the lead. Blanche, however, when she first joined the company, was not particularly interested in her film work. When Griffith invited her to come out to California with the company, she turned him down, preferring to embark on a dancing tour with Gertrude Hoffman.

The Biograph film with which Blanche will always be identified is, of course, *The Lonedale Operator*, released March 23, 1911, but I prefer to discuss in this essay two of her other pictures, *Oil and Water*, released February 6, 1913, and *The Painted Lady*, released October 24, 1912. In each Blanche gives outstanding performances.

Oil and Water has her as a dancer, wooed by Henry B. Walthall. She gives up the stage in order to marry him and have a child, but later in the film she gives up both her husband and her child in order to return to the stage, her love for which she can never lose. One title describes her as "a great actress both offstage and on," and this is precisely what Blanche's gestures indicate. In every movement, she is the great stage actress, and this from a girl in her mid-teens.

"I can remember *Oil and Water* because Griffith was trying for something, a characterisation. You didn't usually have time for characterisations in pictures in those days, because you got through as quickly as you could do it adequately. I mean you did the best you could, but you couldn't take time. We had a system, if anything could be called a system in those days. For instance, we were supposed to do exteriors, and it was raining or snowing, and we couldn't do them. Then, we would take that day to stay inside and rehearse several ideas, not just one but several, so that we would have a backlog on which to draw when something happened like inclement weather. Then we could go right into shooting in the studio. I don't know if other directors did that or not, but that was his way of doing it."

The Painted Lady I personally feel was one of Biograph's finest releases. Miss Sweet portrays a young girl who, unlike her sister, scorns paint and powder for her face. But it is her sister who attracts the men, until one day a young man comes along who appears to have genuine affection for Blanche. It subsequently transpires that the reason for his affection was his interest in the contents of her father's safe. The night he breaks in the house, Blanche is awakened, takes a gun, and goes downstairs to investigate. She comes upon a masked

Judith of Bethulia: Judith (Blanche Sweet) entertains Holofernes (Henry B. Walthall)

intruder, shoots him and then, removing the mask, discovers his true identity. The girl gradually succumbs to madness, making visits to a bridge where she had once met her lover. Each time her mother, Kate Bruce, brings her back home. Then, one fateful day, the mother falls asleep. Blanche goes to her sister's room, applies powder and paint, and makes a last visit to the old trysting place. There her parents discover her, as the girl falls dead in their arms.

This psychological drama contains one of the most moving performances by any actress from the cinema's infancy. Blanche's every movement is perfectly in keeping with the emotion of the moment. After she has fired a shot at the intruder and he has fallen down, she pleads with him to get up and then, hesitantly, removes his mask and then, as she realises the dreadful truth, collapses. At each visit to the bridge, we know, or we think we know, every word that the girl speaks.

The Painted Lady was singled out by the *New York Dramatic Mirror* for particular attention. "A scenario editor trained to work in a groove would have balked at the script, a director of less keen perceptions would have insisted on more conventional acting, and a woman less thoroughly an artist would have spoiled the picture. If proof is required, the picture shows that producers need not confine themselves to the stupidly obvious, also that fine shades of mental suffering may be communicated to an audience through the medium of a photoplay. Skilled acting is the chief requisite and the Biograph Company has at least one actress capable of delicately shaded work."

By 1912, Blanche Sweet was being recognised as one of the screen's finest dramatic actresses, if not *the* finest. And all the while, her name remained unknown to the filmgoing public. "I don't know whether we cared or not," says Blanche, "I can't remember mourning the fact."

Aside from her films for Griffith at Biograph, Blanche also appeared in two films directed by Wilfred Lucas, and shot in Canada. With Mary Pickford and Mack Sennett, she was also in Frank Powell's directorial debut, *All on Account of the Milk,* released January 13, 1910. For a first work, it was very favourably received. *Moving Picture World* commented, "This little comedy is to be commended. It is one of those clean, delicious bits that amuse, and at the same time arouse the imagination of those who see the picture, influencing them to read into it all sorts of pleasant features which perhaps do not appear on the screen."

During 1913, Miss Sweet appeared in a number of Biograph releases nominally supervised by Griffith ("As far as supervision goes, you hardly knew he was in the studio at that time"), but directed by,

Blanche Sweet in *The Fighting Cressy*

among others, James Kirkwood. Typical of these productions is Kirkwood's *Strongheart,* a two-reeler featuring Henry B. Walthall as the son of an Indian chief who falls in love with Blanche. The film ends, as one might expect, with Blanche realising the Indian race would not accept her, and Walthall realising the same thing about himself

and the white race. *Strongheart,* which is rather a confused film because of a sub-plot involving stolen signals for a football game, is
interesting in that it shows how lost Blanche was at this time without
Griffith's guiding hand. She wanders through the film looking totally
bored, and whenever any display of emotion is required from her,
her answer is to play around with a wretched flower.

To close Miss Sweet's career at American Biograph, it is appropriate to discuss *Judith of Bethulia,* which, although filmed in 1913,
was not released until after Griffith had left Biograph, on March 8,
1914. Blanche's performance in the title role was one of the early
American cinema's supreme acting achievements. Her portrayal of
Judith, who is prepared to sacrifice herself to Holofernes to ensure
the safety and happiness of her people, is faultless. The film was
based on a stage play by Thomas Bailey Aldrich, and had been
adapted by Frank Woods; Vachel Lindsay in his *The Art of the
Moving Picture* described it as one of the "two most significant photo-
plays I have ever encountered." The role was played on the stage by
Nance O'Neil, but it is doubtful if any stage actors equalled Blanche
Sweet and Henry B. Walthall (as Holofernes) in this challenge of
beauty against strength.

The play, *Judith of Bethulia,* was written for Miss O'Neil by
Thomas Bailey Aldrich from his poem, "Judith and Holofernes."
Nance O'Neil had already played in his *Mercedes.* The play received
a mixed reception; it was liked in Boston, but not in New York.

"I don't know why he picked *Judith,* except that it was a wonderful
story. It had one thing against it—that it had a tragic ending, which
was *verboten.* Maybe it was because *Quo Vadis* had been released.

"My story is that we saw it together. Now, I'm not a liar, but
inadvertently I could be one. I got to be a little worried about this
story; most people say that he did not see it. That worried me. So
they ran *Quo Vadis* over at Modern Art [The Museum of Modern
Art] one day, and I went over to see it, to see if there was anything
he could have lifted, or taken out of it, or followed, or copied, or
anything. There wasn't a thing! It was just a lot of bad acting, a lot
of very exaggerated acting. We were still exaggerating a little, but
not anything like that. That was all there was to it, except there was
a high wall, the chariot race, and there was a depth to the sets, there
was a vista. We'd had vistas, goodness knows: you made a Western,
you couldn't do it without a vista! They had vistas in their studio
scenes. We didn't have any vistas in our interiors; we didn't have
enough studio space. We did have a high wall. We thought it was
the highest wall ever built; of course, he doubled it afterwards."

Judith of Bethulia was universally acclaimed. In America, *Moving Picture World* described it as "a fascinating work of high artistry . . . an encouraging step in the development of the new art." In England, *The Morning Advertiser* declared it "must surely be the limit of storytelling by moving pictures." *The Times* thought it "almost too realistic," and *Jewish World* wrote, "Thus does the cinematograph pierce with light the darkness of time."

In 1927, Andre Beranger arranged a Hollywood party at which he screened "old" films from his collection for, among others, Laura La Plante, Lois Wilson and Carmelita Geraghty. Among the films was *Judith of Bethulia,* and a gossip columnist from *Picture Play,* present at the party, noted, "Blanche Sweet was a revelation in her potent dramatic power and personal beauty." So little had screen acting progressed—if it has ever progressed—since Blanche's performance in 1913.

Griffith had planned to film *Salambo* for Biograph after completion of *Judith of Bethulia.* Instead, he accepted a contract with Reliance-Majestic, and took with him virtually all his players from *Judith,* with the inexplicable exception of Kate Bruce, who had played Judith's maid.

Blanche Sweet recalls telling the studio she was leaving. "There was a man called Hunter, or Hunter something, and he was a Klaw and Erlanger man. [Klaw and Erlanger by this time had business interests in American Biograph.] He was the one I had to go to and say I was leaving, which I did. He was outraged. He said, 'You can't go.' I said, 'I'm sorry, but I have no contract with the company; I can do just as I please, and I please to go.' All I could think of was I mustn't let him talk me in or out of anything, that all I must say was 'No, No, No,' and get out. Then I started to go, and he started following me, and sort of grabbing at me. Then he started calling at me—and his favourite word was 'maggot.' He started shouting at me, 'You maggot, you.' And I started running, and I almost got to the door, then he got in front of me. So here we were going round the table, running as fast as we both could. I got out the door anyway, and out of the studio."

For his films at Reliance-Majestic, Griffith rented space on East 23rd Street. "It was just a loft, or very close to it." Blanche was to make only three films for the company, and they were to be her last with D. W. Grffiith. She began work on *The Escape,* based on the famous stage play by Paul Armstrong; Blanche was to play the lead, supported by Mae Marsh, Donald Crisp, and Robert Harron.

However, work had no sooner begun on the film when Blanche was

Anna Christie: Blanche Sweet in the title role

Anna Christie: The first meeting between Anna (Blanche Sweet) and her father (George Marion)

taken ill with scarlet fever, caused by her contact with old clothing that had not been properly cleaned. "We started the picture, and the beginning of it is a tenement sequence in which Mae and I are sewing, making clothes or something. We are in old dilapidated clothes, and we had gone and picked them out, not at a thrift shop, nothing as good as a thrift shop, but at some old rag place." Griffith postponed shooting on the picture, and instead put *The Battle of the Sexes* into production.

"You see, I'd spoiled everything. I was in trouble. Everybody hated me. I hated myself. After my four weeks was over, I crept out to California, afraid to face everybody because I had wrecked everything. I was innocent enough, but . . ."

After *The Escape* came *Home Sweet Home,* also produced in 1914. Suggested by the life of John Howard Payne, *Home Sweet Home* showed how Payne's song had been a steadying and guiding influence in the lives of various people, depicted in the three stories, which, with the prologue and epilogue, made up the film. The opening title explained: "Not biographical but photo-dramatic and allegorical, and might apply [*sic.*] to the lives and works of many men of genius, whose failings in private life have been outweighed by their great gifts to humanity."

Blanche played a leading role in the third story, which opens with her wedding to Courtney Foote, during which the two hear a lovesick boy playing "Home Sweet Home" on the violin. Time passes. The husband goes off to his club, and while he is away, Blanche is visited and tempted to adultery by Owen Moore. The husband returns, but decides to finish his cigar before entering his wife's room, and in so doing falls asleep. Blanche has almost decided to leave with Moore when she hears a man across the street playing "Home Sweet Home" on his violin for her maid. The music works its spell, and Blanche turns the tempter away. A title "Ten Years Later" precedes a shot of Blanche and Foote sitting with a child on each knee; a third child enters and kneels to pray.

Subtitled "The Marriage of Roses and Lilies," this story is not the best episode in the picture; that distinction belongs to the Mae Marsh-Robert Harron sequence. It is, however, a charming little tale, nicely played although with no great acting required from any of the principals.

Blanche's third feature-length film of 1914 was *The Avenging Conscience,* based on two short stories by Edgar Allan Poe, "The Tell-Tale Heart" and "The Pit and the Pendulum," and his poem, "Annabel Lee." Blanche played Annabel, loved by Henry B. Wal-

Anna Christie: Blanche Sweet and William Russell

thall, who says, to her, "In your voice I hear Pan playing in the woods and all the world gives heed." It is for her that Walthall kills his uncle (Spottiswoode Aitken), who will not consent to a wedding or part with any of his money. However, after various mildly horrific moments, it all proves to have been a dream. Criticism was mixed. As far as the *Syracuse Post Standard* was concerned, "It preaches

Blanche Sweet and Bessie Love display their musical talents in *Those Who Dance*

nothing in particular, unless it be that it is wrong to choke an un-offending uncle to death to get his money." But *Reel Life* was more serious in its approach: "For the first time in the history of the motion picture the weird imaginative genius of Edgar Allan Poe has been made captive for the screens and by the master hand of the world's foremost exponent of the motion picture art. . . . Its lesson is vivid, convincing, and intensely realistic, epitomizing in motion picture form Poe's own idea of the psychology of conscience."

When Blanche arrived in California to complete *The Escape,* it was already common knowledge that Griffith was planning to film Thomas Dixon's *The Clansman.* It seemed obvious casting for Blanche to play Elsie Stoneman. But while *The Birth of a Nation* was in pre-production planning stages, Blanche was approached by Jesse L. Lasky and Cecil B. DeMille and asked to join their newly formed company, "after an exhaustive study of the characteristics and abili-ties of all the more widely known young women now appearing in photo-plays," as the original press release stated.

"I went to Griffith and told him, and expected him to say 'No, I need you.' And he didn't; he told me to go. I was disappointed and very hurt, because I didn't want to go. I was afraid to go. Mary [Pickford] said somewhere that when she said she was going, he just blessed her and said, 'I'll miss you—I hope everything goes well.' But he didn't do that with me. He certainly didn't bless me, and he didn't hope for anything. He just said he thought I was capable of doing it, and he never got in touch with me afterwards, which I felt he should have done, and I hoped for. He never said that he saw certain pictures, and that I was good, or I could be doing better. I went back, I guess, in a few months, or it may have been a year, I can't remember. All I know is that the *Intolerance* sets were going up. I went back to the studios, and visited with the ones I knew well, and then Griffith came along. He took me across the street to see the sets for *Intolerance,* and I know his motive was to impress me, and he certainly did. And I thought, 'Oh, I wish I was working on that.' I didn't say that, but I wished that."

Why Griffith let Blanche go, no one will ever know; it hardly seems credible that he could so easily have said farewell to an actress who *Moving Picture World* had called, a year earlier, "one of the greatest emotional actresses in the silent drama." Perhaps Griffith thought that Blanche had given all she could emotionally to his films; if so, then her later work proves that Griffith was wrong. Or perhaps he was just happy that his "children" should be so desired by other companies and become so successful—if a high salary is a sign of success.

Blanche Sweet vividly recalled how Griffith would rehearse a scene with his players:

"He would have an idea, maybe it was his own idea, maybe something he bought, and say, 'This is the idea of the film.' And then you'd start elaborating—you see somebody there, you talk to somebody, you kill somebody. I mean whatever it was. And you started improvising and doing it as you thought it should be done, or could be done. And, if it was all right, good. But, if it wasn't, he'd say, 'No, I think let's do something else.' And he might tell you what to do, but if that didn't start opening it up, he'd get up and show you. And that's really what he did—it pulverised you. Because he wasn't a good actor on the stage; I understand he wasn't a good actor in the few films that he made early, but he was a magnificent actor as a director—simply wonderful. I've never seen better acting on anybody's part. He could do a woman just as perfectly as he could do a man's part. And he would do it so well that you were simply crushed,

and you would say 'I can't do it.' And then you'd start pulling your-
self together, and try to do it just as well as you could along the line
that he had suggested, but that's an awfully hard thing to follow—
somebody who does something awfully well."

When I talked to Bessie Love on the same subject, she echoed
Blanche's words, exclaiming "He inspired you so."

Blanche's first film for Lasky, *The Warrens of Virginia*, released
only days after the first screening of *The Birth of a Nation*, was a
major triumph for both its star and its director, Cecil B. DeMille.
Based on a play by William C. de Mille, the film also dealt with the
American Civil War, but with one particular incident in the war, the
love of the daughter of a Confederate general (Blanche) for a Union
lieutenant (House Peters). It must have been strange for DeMille
to be directing a film based on a stage play in which he had once
played a small role. However, DeMille handles his actors, with the
possible exception of House Peters, splendidly, and the battle scenes
show that Griffith was to have a serious rival in DeMille, even at
this early time. There is a quality of belief running through Blanche's
performance that proves she was perfectly at home working under
a director other than Griffith.

Miss Sweet herself, however, was not too happy with the film or
her performance. "I had a terrible time—so did Cecil. I was terrified
of him for many reasons. I had never worked with any other director,
except for one or two things, except Griffith. And here I was going
out on my own. Whatever I did had to be me and nobody else. And
here I was with a strange director that I didn't know anything about.
His version of the story was that he was terrified of me. He was
working with a Griffith player, who was supposed to have quite a
reputation, and he didn't know very much about films himself. And
here the two of us sat staring at each other. Afterwards he said, 'You
know, you used to give me these hard looks. I thought you were
saying, this man doesn't know what he's talking about.' And I said,
'No, on the contrary, Cecil, I was looking attentively at you, trying
to find out what you wanted from me, what your conception of the
story, of a scene, was. I was trying to understand you, and therefore,
I was looking as hard as I could into your eyes, trying to interpret
your eyes.' No, we didn't get along, unfortunately. We just didn't
spark each other." It was this probably that caused the director to
make only one more film with Blanche—*The Captive*, also released
in 1915.

Tess of the d'Urbervilles: Blanche Sweet and Conrad Nagel

The following year Miss Sweet made three films with Cecil's brother William, and here she found a more sensitive director. William de Mille was also more taken with Blanche than his brother had been. In his autobiography he wrote about his first film with Blanche, *The Ragamuffin*, which was also his debut as a director: "I considered myself lucky to have so good a star for my first directorial venture." "We seemed to have more accord about the way we worked," recalls Blanche.

The last three films under Blanche's Lasky contract were directed by Marshall Neilan, whom she was to marry in 1922. The couple had first met at American Biograph, where Neilan was working as an actor. "I don't think Marshall amounted to very much as an actor; he was passable, good-looking, and as good as a lot of them. But he had ideas; he was intelligent and he had ideas about doing things. The ideas were always a little ahead and a little advanced. Liking his ideas about producing and so forth, I went to Cecil B. DeMille and said, 'I would like to have you get this young man as the director of my next film.' And we argued for a while, and then he said, 'Well, all right.' "

After leaving Lasky because of a failure to agree upon a satisfactory contract, Blanche was away from the screen for two years. She became hostile and cynical, and went through a very temperamental period which precluded any film work. Harry Carr wrote of her, "She was an extremely difficult and disagreeable girl—about nine-tenths of the time. She went out of her way to insult newspaper critics. Very few directors would work with her." (13) Adela Rogers St. Johns wrote that Blanche reminded her of the famous line by Kipling, about the woman who "had known all the sorrow in the world and was laughing at it." (48)

Between 1919 and 1923, Miss Sweet appeared in a series of what can only be described as unimportant program pictures. A typical critical reaction was "Blanche Sweet's acting lifts up average plot" (*Motion Picture News*). But as Blanche points out, "Supposedly, but

A perfectly composed shot of Blanche Sweet and the children in *Tess of the d'Urbervilles*

it doesn't. It just doesn't. I made a series of things, just what I shouldn't have done. I made three or four pictures a year, none of them any good really." Typical of such films was Wallace Worsley's *A Woman of Pleasure* (1919). "I can't remember that. It must have been bad for me to have forgotten it so completely."

Blanche had returned to the screen in Marshall Neilan's *The Unpardonable Sin,* but it was her third production of 1919, *Fighting Cressy,* which the critics liked. *Photoplay* (March, 1920) said, "Blanche Sweet has come back to the screen after an absence of two years with deepened powers, a Blanche Sweet full of 'McKinstry pride,' quick at the trigger, quick to hate or love, full of fire—and lovelier than the old days." Miss Sweet recalls, "I had a very lovely feeling about doing a Bret Harte story. I loved Bret Harte stories, because he had a knowledge of the West, of pioneer days, of early America that was very close and very dear to me." Directed by Robert Thornby, the film has Blanche as a gun-toting Western girl who single-handedly ends a feud between her family, the McKinstrys, and the Harrisons.

Two other films that Blanche liked from this period were Henry King's *Help Wanted—Male* (1920), in which Blanche portrayed a telephone operator who inherits $1,000 and secures herself a husband (the leading man, played by director King), and Clarence Badger's *Quincy Adams Sawyer* (1922).

Blanche enjoyed playing in *Help Wanted—Male* for one very good reason. "This was a light comedy. I used to complain so about not being given any comedies, because they seemed to think the public wanted—and therefore they wanted—dramas. And I had done so many dramatic things that it wasn't right, it wasn't good for me. It was a bore. After all, you get very tired of doing a lot of tragic things exclusively. So after I bullied and begged I'd get a comedy occasionally. I don't think I made any remarkable impression, but for me it was very good." She did, however, make an impression with the critic of *Photoplay* (September, 1920). "Blanche makes herself over; she is not languorous, but energetic; she sprints on the sands; she runs races with a dog; she is a sort of devilish combination of Constance Talmadge and Dorothy Gish."

Of *Quincy Adams Sawyer,* Blanche says, "I enjoyed doing that. We made it up on the Columbia River, near Washington. I loved making outdoor films, that I enjoyed more than anything I think. It was something partially like *Way Down East*—the same situation. It

Publicity portrait of Blanche Sweet released in connection with *The Woman in White*

was a very cold river. I don't think it was as cold as they were in the East, but it was cold enough. I was wet all day long. They would get buckets of water. When I wasn't in the water, when I was on the boat, I was just drenched constantly. And I said, the first day we were going to go into this sequence, 'Now I know I'm going to be cold and wet all day, so I wish you would go and get a bottle of whiskey, and come late afternoon, when I'm getting a little weary, and colder and colder, I may need to have a drink of whiskey to warm me up.' So came the afternoon's work, I noticed everyone was getting so genial and having so much fun, and here I was shivering and thinking, 'Towards the end of the day, I'll be able to have a drink of whiskey, and I'll be all right; it'll warm me up.' And came the end of the day, there wasn't a drop in the bottle. That was what was making the crew so merry!"

For the film, Blanche was joined by an excellent group of principals—Lon Chaney, John Bowers, and Barbara La Marr—and an outstanding group of supporting players, including Victor Potel, Gale Henry, Louise Fazenda, and Claire McDowell. Miss Sweet confirms what many people have written in describing Badger as "an excellent director."

Then, in 1923, Blanche began work on what was undoubtedly her most important film of the twenties, if not the most important film of her entire career, *Anna Christie*. Produced by Thomas Ince for release through First National, and directed by John Griffith Wray, the film was considered lost for many years, until a print was discovered in the Jugoslav Film Archive.

"I knew Tom Ince and his wife and family; we were all friends, and I suppose because I was blonde and looked Swedish, Tom naturally thought of me for Anna. He approached me, I didn't approach him, but I welcomed him with open arms when he told me what he wanted to talk to me about. Of course I hadn't seen the play at that time, but I had read it, and was very enthusiastic about it, because it was a great success on the stage and Eugene O'Neill was our outstanding playwright. I was very eager to do it. It wasn't until months after we finished the film that Pauline Lord, who originated Anna on the stage and was greatly successful in this country and London, came to Los Angeles with the play, and I saw the play. I went backstage later, and said how much I had admired her performance, how beautiful it was, and I said had I ever seen her in the play before I made the picture, I never would have had the courage to do it, and I wouldn't. She was so magnificent in the play, it discouraged you completely. You thought, 'Oh, I could never touch that.' But not having seen it, I dared to go ahead.

"George Marion was the original father of the stage play; he later played it in London, and then he came out to do the version with me, and then he later did it with Garbo. William Russell had never played anything important . . . like an O'Neill play or anything special. He had done a lot of Westerns, did them very well, but that was all. He was big-bodied, and very he-mannish, and that was one reason for asking him to play opposite me, because that was the character of the sailor in *Anna*. He was soaked in the theater, and so dedicated and so enthralled by the fact that he was doing something big and important that he just gave himself heart and soul—and brawn—to the character. And he was wonderful to work with for that reason.

"John Griffith Wray: He again was quite enthralled by his subject, and also worked to make it a fine picture, but his ways were ways that I was not accustomed to. He was a very excitable man, and he would get carried away. So much so that he used a megaphone for a close-up, and, you know, you don't even talk to anybody in a close-up, you don't say a word, they know what to do. And it got a little bit on our nerves. He meant so well; he was so sincere. But that bothered me a little; in fact, we retook some of the scenes. I asked to have them retaken; I wasn't happy about them, and I asked Tom Ince if he would redirect them. But I didn't know that Tom was that excitable too, because he did the same thing.

"It was a great character, a very lovable character. I had one of the greatest compliments of my life paid to me after the picture opened in London. I was over there on a visit, and we went to a nightspot that was sort of fashionable to go to, but which was a most unfashionable place. And there were a lot of prostitutes there, and they recognised me. One of them came over and spoke to me, and said she had enjoyed seeing *Anna Christie* so much, and one by one, these girls came over and sat down at the table—nobody asked them to—they just sat down, and wanted to talk to me. They treated me as if I were one of them, and that I knew all about their lives. They knew all about mine because they'd seen *Anna Christie*. I so appreciated that, because I felt perhaps I had conveyed the spirit of the character."

Ince had some misgivings about the film's box office potential, but *Anna Christie* proved to be both critically and commercially one of the most popular films of 1924. *Motion Picture Classic* (February, 1924) wrote of Blanche's performance, "Blanche Sweet's rendition of the title role is marvellously human. The emotions which race across her face indicate that she lived the part thoroughly. She plays with a remarkable depth of sympathy and understanding." Adele Whitely

Fletcher writing in the February, 1924 issue of *Motion Picture Magazine* gave similar praise. "She has blended crudity, poetry, poignancy and an ironic bitterness in her characterization in a way which wins our unstinted praise. And beyond all this, there are few faces on either the stage or screen which interest us more than Blanche Sweet's. For in her countenance you find an intelligent beauty . . . what is rarer?" The film was, of course, remade in 1930 by Clarence Brown as Garbo's first talkie. It is a tragedy that the role was not again offered to Blanche, but at that time MGM was less interested in the suitability of actresses than in protecting its interests in its biggest star.

After the completion of *Anna Christie,* Blanche made one more film for Thomas Ince, *Those Who Dance,* directed by Lambert Hillyer, and also released in 1924. As her leading man she had Warner Baxter, and costarring was Miss Sweet's closest friend, Bessie Love. She and Bessie had met while Bessie was working under Marshall Neilan's direction on *The Eternal Three* in 1923. Blanche had told Neilan to bring his leading lady to the house, and since that meeting the two had become firm friends.

Blanche recalls, "I admired her work tremendously, so I went to the director, and he was such a nice man and a very good director, and said, 'Look, I want you to give Bessie every break you can in this picture, because she's a wonderful actress. Just give her every advantage.' Well, after a couple of days, I saw the first rushes, and I said, 'Fine, fine,' but I started scrambling because it looked as if Bessie didn't need any breaks, none at all. She just went along, and I thought that I'd better look out, they won't know I'm in the film even!" Bessie told me of a scene towards the end of the production in which she, as the gangster's moll, realised that she could not live without the man she loved, regardless of what he might be. After the scene had been shot, Blanche turned to Bessie and said, "Remind me to tell you how much I hate you for doing that scene so beautifully." The two have never lost touch with one another, and in 1963 Blanche flew to London to take part in the BBC's *This Is Your Life* program featuring Bessie. "I'd go anywhere for Bessie," said Blanche to DeWitt Bodeen. (6)

Those Who Dance was followed later in 1924 by *Tess of the D'Urbervilles,* based on the novel by Thomas Hardy ("another good writer"). The film, now unhappily thought lost, was directed by Marshall Neilan, and the couple, with cameraman David Kesson, went on location to England for over two weeks shooting exteriors.

In England, they also shot scenes for Blanche's next film, *The Sporting Venus,* and for a projected film based on Rebecca West's *The Return of the Soldier.* "I talked the book into being as a film. I had bought it. We talked many times with Rebecca West, but we never finished the film." While the couple were away from Metro-Goldwyn, with whom they had a releasing arrangement, the amalgamation with Louis B. Mayer's organisation took place, and, as Blanche points out, "Louis B. Mayer and Marshall Neilan were just naturally born enemies." On their return, endless litigation began. "Everybody was suing everybody else, and it was a very unpleasant time, and we never did finish the picture. Later Warner Brothers bought it from me for Bette Davis to do, but they never made it. It's never been made and never will be made because it was a war story, a fictional war story, and you just don't do that anymore. We're trying to get away from war subjects."

In 1925, Blanche went to First National, an organisation for which

Blanche Sweet asks assistant director Herman Bing for work in *Showgirl in Hollywood*

she had great respect and for which she enjoyed working, to play opposite Ronald Colman (who had also been her leading man in *The Sporting Venus*) in *His Supreme Moment,* directed by George Fitzmaurice. "He was a fine director, and he was fun to work with." She followed *His Supreme Moment* with seven films in two years; none of them did anything for her career, and to all intents and purposes they were a total waste of her talent.

Not only was Blanche's film career getting into a rut, but her personal life was far from happy, and in 1929 she went to Paris in order to obtain a divorce from Neilan. While there, she was approached by Herbert Wilcox, who asked her to come, as he had Mae Marsh and Dorothy Gish before her, to England to star in a picture. Wilcox chose for Blanche *The Woman in White,* based on the popular novel by Wilkie Collins.

"Of course that was a catastrophe; it was simply dreadful for poor Herbert, and I liked him so much as a man and as a director. Just as we finished it sound came in, and there we were stuck with a silent picture. I don't think it was sent over here, because nobody wanted anything but sound.

"I remember on my way back, I stopped over in Chicago, and I rushed in to see my first talking picture. I didn't know what it was all about. It was *The Lion and the Mouse,* an old traditional play in film form, with Lionel Barrymore. And I remember one scene, when in a fit of rage he had to sweep a bust off a high pedestal, which he did, and one minute later came the crash. So I said, 'Oh! That's talking pictures!' "

Blanche's first talking role was in a Warner Brothers' Vitaphone short, entitled *Always Faithful,* released in 1929. No information on the short remains in the files of Warner Brothers, and Miss Sweet's comment is "I don't remember a thing about that; I've never ever seen it." She followed this in 1930 with *The Woman Racket,* directed by Robert Ober and Albert Kelley for MGM.

Then, in the same year, she was back at First National for Mervyn LeRoy's *Showgirl in Hollywood,* featuring Jack Mulhall and Alice White. "I was not particularly happy with it," says Blanche. "I'd known Mervyn LeRoy for a long time, and I let him influence me. He just talked me into it."

Miss Sweet portrays a onetime silent star, now unable to obtain work, who befriends a young showgirl, played with a remarkable lack of talent by Alice White. After a heart-to-heart talk between the two on the life of an actress in the film capital of the world, Blanche

Blanche Sweet with Raymond Hackett at their wedding

sings the poignant "There's a Tear for Every Smile in Hollywood."
The film also contains a very moving tribute to the art of the silent
screen, and a tribute to Blanche's talent as an exponent of what was
now a vanished art. Alice White, as Dixie Dugan, has given Blanche
a part in her new production—a chance at a comeback—but because
of White's temperamental outbursts production has been suspended.
Blanche stands looking out from one of the windows of her home,
tears running down her face. She slowly walks down the stairs, goes
to her desk, and takes out a phial of poison. The old chauffeur breaks
the silence by asking if she needs the car to go to the studio. "No,"
replies Blanche, "I shan't be going to the studio any more."

She did return to the studio, to RKO, for one last film, *The Silver
Horde,* directed by George Archainbaud. Then she left Hollywood
and, under the auspices of Max Gordon, toured in vaudeville with
an act entitled "Sweet and Lovely." In 1935, Blanche played on
Broadway in Robert Sherwood's *The Petrified Forest.* Arthur Hopkins was the director, and her costars were Humphrey Bogart and
Leslie Howard.

So committed to the theater had Blanche become that, during the
run of the play, she had to turn down an offer from MGM. She
appeared in several plays with Raymond Hackett, whom she married
in 1936. The couple had met while Hackett was starring at MGM
in the early thirties. It was a happy and a lasting marriage, which
only broke up with Raymond's death in 1958; Blanche has described
their years together as "the happiest of my life." Today, she is still
proud to be known as Mrs. Raymond Hackett.

In 1948, the couple returned to California, and Blanche retired
from the stage. "I'd go back any second if I got something good. I can
look back and say I've had my share. There are some things I wish
I hadn't done. There was one picture, *The Lady from Hell* [1926],
I did because they offered me $10,000 a week. I would never after
that do the same thing again—for money it isn't worth it. Let's rest
on the record. I feel I can go on my record."

In 1915, Griffith described Blanche Sweet as the most natural actress in filmdom. (36) Her career more than justifies his estimation
of her.

4

Mary Pickford

I pleased my own generation—
that is all that matters.
—Mary Pickford

There is a scene in Douglas Fairbanks's *The Gaucho* (1927) in which Mary Pickford appears as the Divine Vision, and as the years have slipped by since Mary's retirement from the screen, this has come to be accepted as the Pickford image—a divine vision radiating sweetness and light. But, of course, this is not the real Mary Pickford, and only now, with the revival of her films by the American Film Institute and George Eastman House, have the two generations that grew up since she was the "most popular woman in the world" had the opportunity of seeing for themselves just how fine an actress and comedienne she was.

Sadly, in some ways this revival has come too late. Miss Pickford herself prefers, for reasons best known to her, to remain closeted in Pickfair, rather than receive the adulation of her new, young admirers. And despite her newfound popularity in the States, in Britain she belongs quite definitely to the past, and her films play at London's National Film Theatre to half-empty houses. The blame for this must rest on the shoulders of Miss Pickford alone; she was wrong when she said in *Photoplay* (May 1931) that pleasing her own gen-

Mary Pickford

eration was all that mattered. That is not all that matters. If Miss Pickford had made her films more available the sentiments of the little poem written by one of her fans for *Picturegoer* (September 1922) would still remain valid.

Though fashion changeth ever so,
Our Mary changeth never,
For stars may come and stars may go,
But she goes on for ever.

What then is the real Mary Pickford? It's a very difficult question to answer for, as Edward Wagenknecht has written, "Her films encourage, and submit to, little analysis." Even as early as 1916, a reviewer in the *New York Dramatic Mirror* commented: "To analyze the acting of Mary Pickford is about as satisfactory as trying to draw a definite conclusion from a metaphysical premise. After much circumlocution, after the use of many words and the expenditure of much grey matter one is forced to the inevitable conclusion that Mary Pickford is Mary Pickford. She has a charm, a manner, an expression that is all her own. She seems to have the happy faculty of becoming for the time being the character she is portraying. At no time does one gather the impression that Mary Pickford is acting. She is the epitome of naturalness. But why go on? The sum and substance of it all is that Mary Pickford is unique, and irrespective of the strength or weakness of any picture in which she appears, the fact that Mary Pickford appears in it makes it a good picture."*

The facts of her life and career are straightforward enough. She was born Gladys Smith in Toronto on April 8, 1893; she made her stage debut at the age of five, adopting the name of Mary Pickford at the suggestion of David Belasco in 1907. (B. P. Schulberg, in a periodical with the unlikely name of *Truth Magazine,* gives a romantic version of why the name Pickford was chosen. "When I asked her mother Charlotte Smith how she came to choose this name for Mary, she told me that when they came down from Toronto to seek stage parts for the child actress, people told her that Gladys Smith lacked glamor as a stage name. They tried for a long time to think of an arresting name for Mary, and once between one-night stands they passed one of the earlier Fords. 'Let's pick Ford,' Charlotte said, and thus was christened one of the great stellar personalities of a new entertainment medium.")

In 1909, she joined the Biograph Company and D. W. Griffith, with whom she had a far from placid relationship; they had many disagreements over billing, parts, and, above all, salary. Of all the

---

* In recent years this review of *Poor Little Peppina* has been quoted many times. To give credit where credit is due, it was first brought to light through the researches of George Pratt, who drew it to the attention of James Card, who subsequently reprinted it in his article "The Films of Mary Pickford" (*Image,* Rochester, N.Y., December 1959), incidentally one of the most important articles yet written on the star.

Mary Pickford with Wilfred Lucas and Kate Bruce in *Home Folks,* a typical
American Biograph subject, released June 6, 1912 (frame enlargement)

Mary Pickford as the mischievous *Rebecca of Sunnybrook Farm*

Stella Maris: Mary Pickford as Unity Blake

actors and actresses whose film careers began with D. W. Griffith, Mary Pickford is the one who is least associated with him, and whose personality was probably far stronger than Griffith's, thus assuring her of giving a good performance no matter under whose direction or how poor the film. Although Miss Pickford was with Griffith for a period of little more than two years (with an unhappy

Stella Maris: Unity Blake entertains the orphans

period with the Imp Company sandwiched between), she has always been eager to point out the debt that she owed to him. In her autobiography she wrote that "I learned more about acting under Griffith's guidance than I did in all my years in the theater," (38) and at the time of his death she said, "To the men and women who were fortunate enough to work with him, he will always be cherished as the man who produced and directed great motion pictures straight from the heart. A flame of perfectionism burned within him, and made him refuse to accept the second-rate from himself or his co-workers. A poet who sang his song in celluloid . . . he had visions of great accomplishments for the medium, and he imparted his faith to others." (40) If Miss Pickford's continued career in movies was in any way the result of a faith imparted to her by Griffith, we have much to thank him for.

The picture-going public and the critics were quick to recognize her talent in her Biograph shorts. *They Would Elope* was a half-reeler shot in July, 1909, a comedy in which she and Billy Quirk decide to elope much to the delight of her family; it was told without titles apart from a shot of a note announcing the intention of the couple to elope. Of this short the *New York Dramatic Mirror* (August 21, 1909) wrote, "This delicious comedy introduced again an ingenue whose work in Biograph pictures is attracting attention." A provincial English newspaper, the *Letchworth Citizen* (June 25, 1910) commented that "Each film-making firm has its own special favourites, and one of the most known at our own Picture Palace is she who takes the leading part in all the films of the American Biograph Company. From gay to grave, the quick flash of her eyes transports us, and many a lesson has she taught us by means of the characters she portrays."

But it is to her features that one must look to see just how talented Mary Pickford was, and one need look no further than *Stella Maris,* directed by Marshall Neilan in 1918. Neilan, one of the most underrated of silent directors, had been Mary's leading man in *Rags, A Girl of Yesterday,* and *Madame Butterfly,* all released during 1915, and directed her in *Rebecca of Sunnybrook Farm* and *A Little Princess* (both 1917), *Stella Maris, Amarilly of Clothes-Line Alley,* and *M'Liss* (all 1918), *Daddy-Long-Legs* (1919), and *Dorothy Vernon*

Stella Maris: Mary Pickford in the title role, with Conway Tearle

Pollyanna: Mary Pickford with Katherine Griffith

of Haddon Hall (1924). Of Neilan's relationship to Miss Pickford, her husband Charles "Buddy" Rogers recalled, "I think she loved him very much—as a friend, as a pal, as a director, as an actor, as a musician. She thought he was a great all-round man. I know it was very sad; we went to his funeral. It was the first time that I've ever gone to a drinking wake. He left money for us all to go back to his favorite bar and play his music and have a rip-roaring time." Neilan died on October 27, 1958; Mary Pickford is always said to have paid for his funeral, although Rogers denied it.

In *Stella Maris*, we first see Mary in the title role as a young girl, suffering from an undefined illness, and "tenderly shielded from all the sordidness and misery of the world." Here is the Mary Pickford we've all read about in the past—a combination of curls and smiles. Next we see her as Unity Blake, an orphan child, and here is a totally different and unexpected Pickford, deformed in her ugliness, putting on a brave and cheerful face despite adversities, but totally unlike the whimpering, sniveling brats of some of Lillian Gish's characterisa-

Sparrows: Mary Pickford proves more than a match for the bullying son of the owner of the baby farm

tions. Adopted by a drunker foster mother (brilliantly portrayed by Marcia Manon—what a great pity this fine actress never appeared in a Griffith feature) who beats her with a poker, Unity falls in love with the woman's estranged husband, but in order that he may be free to marry Stella Maris, she eventually kills both her foster mother and herself. The film has moments of extreme violence, as when Pickford is beaten, but it also has moments of great tenderness, as when Unity learns she is to be adopted or when she makes love to Conway Tearle's jacket, and in the scenes in the garden between Tearle and Stella Maris. And above all there is comedy.

Comedy was always an integral part of a Pickford feature. In *Pollyanna,* adapted from a book overladen with nauseating sentimentality, there are moments of superb comedy; Mary catches a fly, asks if it wants to go to heaven, squashes it on the table, and announces, "Well, you have." In *Rebecca of Sunnybrook Farm,* about to steal some food from the kitchen, she is nonplussed to read two signs on

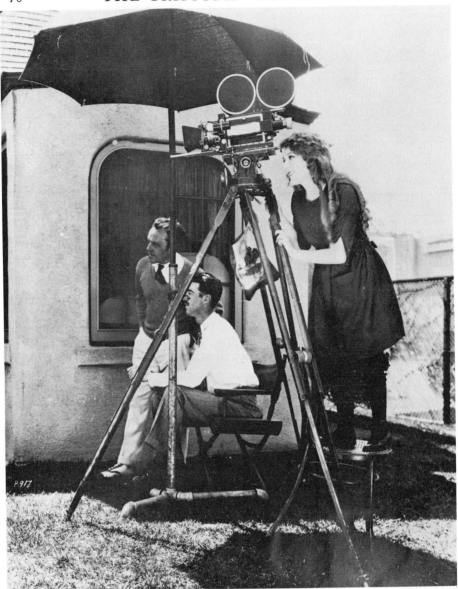

Little Annie Rooney (1925): Star Mary Pickford with cameraman Charles Rosher and director William Beaudine

opposite walls: "Thou shalt not steal" and "The Lord helps those who help themselves."

In *Sparrows* (1926), one of the most moving of Pickford vehicles, with sentiment kept to a minimum and firmly under the control of director William Beaudine, there is much comedy, such as the scene

My Best Girl: Mary Pickford has Buddy Rogers at her feet

where one of the "orphants" nearly loses his trousers during the
crossing of the swamp, or the frequent, and amusing, appeals to God
from His "Sparrows." But it would be wrong to write about *Sparrows* without mentioning the far from comic scene of the death of the
baby. Here surely is one of the greatest moments in any silent picture;

the restraint of Miss Pickford's performance as she gradually realises
that the baby is dead, the superimposition of a hillside on the wall of
the barn, and Christ's coming from that hillside to take the baby
from Mary into His arms—this is a sequence that will live in the
memories of all who have seen *Sparrows*. In its own way it makes the
teachings of Christ more believable than any sermon preached from
a pulpit.

The mixing of comedy and pathos, usually around the motif of
self-sacrifice, was typical of virtually all the Pickford features. In
My Best Girl, when she realises that she may not be a good enough
wife for "Buddy" Rogers, she is prepared to have his father (played
with a typically fine performance by Hobart Bosworth) believe her
to be a "flapper" interested only in how much money she can make.
"That's me all over—a red hot mama." In this film even the comic
moments with the family contain elements of self-sacrifice. Whenever
a member of the family is in any sort of trouble, the cry goes out—as
when the sister is arrested by the police—"Where's Maggie, can't
she do something about it?" It is perhaps interesting to note that
Close Up (March 1928) considered *My Best Girl* a better film than
Murnau's *Sunrise*. "In that film, if one took away what Pickford
stands for (Good Wifehood, Little Lord Fauntleroy, Gladys Smith
and her Niece and Arrested Development) one got, suddenly, a common couple, very happy, walking through the rain, slashing across
everyone's little bothers with their love. And, of course, all that
Pickford stands for takes itself away."

In *My Best Girl*, Miss Pickford's costar is Charles "Buddy" Rogers, and a title in which she says to him "I may take you in hand and
try and make something out of you" now seems oddly prophetic in
view of their subsequent marriage. (Miss Pickford had previously
been married to Owen Moore and, of course, Douglas Fairbanks.)
Rogers recalled for me how he came to be chosen for *My Best Girl*.

"When we finished *Wings*, I was at a dance one Saturday night,
and a woman who had adapted *Wings* said, 'Buddy, what are you
doing for lunch on Monday?' I said, 'Nothing.' She said, 'I'll meet
you in front of Paramount Studios at twelve o'clock.' I said, 'Fine.'
She drove up in her car, I got in, and we drove to another studio. It
was a new studio to me, and there was a bungalow there. She said,
'Buddy, will you ring the doorbell; I'll park the car.' I rang the bell,
and America's sweetheart with all the curls opened the door. It was
a plot to get me over there to see whether Miss Pickford might think
I might be good for her leading man. As a matter of fact, when I

Mary Pickford and Buddy Rogers: "Maggie, you are my best girl?"

was in college—and she later heard this—I preferred Norma Shearer to her. Didn't go over too well!"

Of working conditions on the Pickford set, Rogers had this to say: "She never threw her power around, I'll say that. Never once in the three or four months that we worked did I hear her make a scene or stop anything. Later on, I believe, she would have meetings at 5:30, 6:00 in the evening and change things around. She was the perfect actress, the perfect friend to work with."

Admittedly, Mary is not always prepared to sacrifice herself. In *The Poor Little Rich Girl* (1917), she throws all her clothes out of a bedroom window rather than allow a spoiled brat to wear one of her dresses. *The Poor Little Rich Girl* was the first feature in which Mary appeared throughout as a young girl, and it set a pattern for all of her subsequent silent films. But she *did* also portray mature women, and any doubt as to her ability to play such roles is dispelled by her performance as Dearest in *Little Lord Fauntleroy* ("Dearest,"

The Taming of the Shrew: Mary Pickford and Douglas Fairbanks

wrote Douglas Fairbanks in 1921, "is Mary as I know her—Mary with unvarying understanding, compassionate, vibrantly the woman.") *Little Lord Fauntleroy* is an excellent example of how Miss Pickford's performance (or in this case, performances, as she portrays both mother and son) can overcome poor material or bad direction.

As to whether Miss Pickford was beginning to become aware of the need for her to play adult roles if her career was to continue and prosper, we can only guess. Perhaps she took note of what Harry

Carr had written in *Motion Picture Magazine*: "At an age when childhood is almost a sad and forgotten memory with most women, Mary can slip away into her locked garden and be a child again. And Mary Pickford knows that the day is coming when her locked garden will be desolate and empty; when she will call for the little girl among the roses and mignonette; but she will never find her."

In her four sound features—*Coquette* (1929), *The Taming of the Shrew* (1929), *Kiki* (1931), and *Secrets* (1933)—she played mature roles, not always with qualified success. In *The Taming of the Shrew* she lacks the spit and fire to make a satisfactory Katherine, but she more than compensates for this by her playing in *Secrets,* where she appears as a teenage girl, a mature woman, and an elderly lady with two grown-up daughters (played by ex-silent stars Ethel Clayton and Bessie Barriscale).

Secrets marked Miss Pickford's retirement from the screen as an actress (she later produced a number of mildly successful pictures). Perhaps she was right to finish when she did, for, after all, the world likes its queens to know when to step down. "You are my Mary, aren't you?" asks Leslie Howard soon after their first meeting in *Secrets,*

Secrets: Mary Pickford and Leslie Howard

Mary Pickford. This photograph was originally published in *Motion Picture Classic* (January 1925) with the caption, "Our Mary looking about fifteen years old as usual!"

and to a whole generation of filmgoers she was their Mary. Like a priestess she was worshiped, and in turn she served as a priestess should. One thing is certain. However many new stars may appear, there will never be another of whom it can be written, as James Shelley Hamilton wrote in *Motion Picture Classic,* "More people look at this face every night than at any other in the world."

5

Dorothy Gish

Oh, she was such fun.
—Bessie Love

"She gives people the impression that she's an awful tomboy," her sister says with a sigh. "I can't help it if I do," the accused replies, "because I do like to climb trees, and I do like to take off my shoes and stockings and go wading, and I do like to swim, and go fishing, and bait my own hooks, and . . ."

"Hush, dear, people will think you're simply terrible and it won't do any good for me to tell them what a perfect darling you are." The last from Miss Lillian Gish to her sister Dorothy. "Mr. Griffith," she remarked, "I've often wondered how the divine Sarah would have played this part." Before Mr. Griffith could answer, Dorothy Gish spoke up: "You mean the great French actress?" she inquired ironically. "Ah yes! She'd do it this way."

The foregoing apocryphal conversation, which appeared in a 1914 issue of *Reel Life,* suggests the essence of Dorothy Gish's personality. Her sense of fun and wit was well-known and appreciated by her many friends. Herbert Wilcox recalls in his autobiography: "The wittiest woman I have met is undoubtedly Dorothy Gish. Whilst in New York I took her to the Pavillon, the smartest and darkest restaurant in the city. About that time a columnist who called herself

77

Dorothy Gish

'Hortense' was dishing out her daily column of poison. 'Hortense' was universally loathed, particularly by her pet target—film stars. Whilst eating, I thought I saw her at a far table, but in the low-key lighting was not certain. 'Isn't that Hortense over there?' I asked. Dorothy looked and without a flicker of a smile answered: 'She looks perfectly relaxed to me.'" (56)

From the day she was born, on March 11, 1898, in Dayton, Ohio, Dorothy's private life was always to be linked with that of her sister. In company with their mother, the two girls spent their early years touring in melodrama, Dorothy having made her stage debut at the age of four. Of her childhood she was to write: "People used to say Lillian would never live to get into her 'teens. She was so quiet and good. I wasn't. I used to get into mischief, and get spanked, and then Lillian cried—so much and so pitifully that she used to make everyone round her do the same." (53) However, there was another side to Dorothy's character, and Lillian recalled that she could be a very serious child, and at times became so serious that she was nicknamed "Grannie Gish."

In 1929, Dorothy reminisced about the plays Lillian and she had worked in as children. "Remember, Lillian, the old Blaney melodrama we used to play in? Remember *Her First False Step*? That was the name of our first melodrama. I always thought it was misnamed. There were two of us; Lillian and I were the false steps. Lillian would run out dressed as a newsboy, and give me a lollypop and I would clap my hands and cry 'Oh Goodie! Goodie!' And Lillian would kneel beside her mother and say, 'Oh mother, what are you doing out here in the cold and snow?' And remember the snow, Lillian? How they used to sweep it up every night and use it again the next day, and we'd have nails and pieces of wood and sometimes dead mice hit us on the head when they threw it down?" (57)

Then, one fateful day in Baltimore, Mrs. Gish took her two young daughters to see a moving picture; it was *Lena and the Geese,* featuring Gladys Smith, whose family was intimate friends of the Gishes. Thus it was that when the Gish family arrived in New York, they went along to the Biograph studios to renew acquaintances with the Smiths, and Gladys, now Mary Pickford, introduced them to D. W. Griffith.

Griffith gave the two girls work as extras at $5 a day, and shortly after the first meeting featured both of them in *An Unseen Enemy,* released September 9, 1912. However, before very long, it became apparent that it was Lillian in whom Griffith was most interested. Linda Arvidson described Dorothy as "a bit too perky to interest the big director." And Griffith told Albert Bigelow Paine, "Dorothy was more apt at getting the director's idea than Lillian, quicker to follow it, more easily satisfied with the result. Lillian conceived an ideal, and patiently sought to realise it."

But it was Dorothy who was the more popular at the studio with the other players. Blanche Sweet recalled: "Dorothy was very close

Hearts of the World: Dorothy Gish and Robert Anderson

I'll Get Him Yet: Dorothy Gish and Richard Barthelmess

Flying Pat (1920) : Dorothy Gish and James Rennie

Another comedy triumph for Dorothy Gish—*Remodeling Her Husband*

and very dear. We got to be excellent friends, and remained so until she died. Griffith asked me, 'Which one do you like?' And I said, 'They're both lovely, they're both beautiful, but I like the younger one. There's something, the expression of her face, it's vivacious.' Lillian was calmer and more placid. Dorothy had humor, of course, for which I have high regard."

Griffith did, however, take Dorothy with him to Reliance-Majestic, perhaps only because Lillian would not have come without her. The director did not use her in either *The Birth of a Nation* or *Intolerance*, but Dorothy was featured in a vast number of Mutual releases directed by, among others, James Kirkwood, Christy Cabanne, and Donald Crisp, all under the nominal supervision of Griffith. Typical of such releases was the 1914 *The Warning*, directed by Donald Crisp.

Dorothy plays Betty, "the wilful, indolent country girl," who likes nothing better than sitting in a hammock, reading popular fiction with doubtful titles such as *The Marriage of Marie*. She is attracted to a drummer from the city, whom she meets outside the local post office, and with whom she elopes. After a fake marriage, the girl rents a dingy tenement room, in which she tries to gas herself. However, the landlady arrives on the scene in time, and sends her home to her mother. But because of her behaviour, her mother tells her to leave. The girl, in abject misery, wanders to a bridge and throws herself into the river. The scene fades, and we see that Dorothy has in fact fallen out of her hammock—it was all a dream. She meets the drummer who had beguiled her with his city manners, tells him she never wants to see him again, and promises her mother that in the future she will be good.

This one-reeler is a delight to watch, and makes one wish that more of Dorothy's pictures from this early period were available for viewing. The range of her acting at such an early date in her career is quite remarkable. It hardly seems believable that comic little Dorothy could play tragedy as finely as she does in the scene of attempted suicide. She stands looking at the gas mantle, turns the gas on, and moves out of frame. All we glimpse is a harrowed, pitiful face, reflected in a mirror by the side of the mantle.

Linda Arvidson at least was aware of her abilities. For she wrote that, while Lillian was watching Dorothy on the set of *The Wife*, released in 1914, the elder sister commented, "Why, Dorothy is good; she's almost as good as I am."* Linda Arvidson continued, "Many more than myself thought Dorothy was better."

* Lillian denies having said this.

Dorothy Gish: A publicity portrait issued in connection with *Orphans of the Storm*

It was Griffith, however, who gave Dorothy her really big chance, when he decided to film *Hearts of the World*. Lillian had already been cast as the heroine, and the role of "The Little Disturber" it was thought would go to Constance Talmadge. However, Lillian

Orphans of the Storm: Lillian and Dorothy Gish

realised that her sister would be ideal for the role, and eventually Griffith was brought around to her way of thinking. Lillian and Mrs. Gish sailed for England in April, 1917, and Dorothy followed two weeks later. Only on her arrival in England—many scenes were shot on location in war-torn France—did Dorothy discover that the role was hers.

Anyone who has seen *Hearts of the World* will remember Dorothy's walk in the picture, and Lillian recalled for me how that walk was discovered. "I was walking with Mr. Griffith in Whitechapel, and we found this girl walking like this, and he said, 'Look at that walk!' And we followed her until she went into a building, and we couldn't any more. And we rushed back. He said, 'Where's your sister? This is a perfect walk for her in this part.' And then we rushed back to the Savoy, and got her, and both of us showed her this walk. And out of that came 'The Little Disturber.' Those little things that you or he or somebody found that would give the key to the character. They have the idea that he sat and told you everything to do. Well,

Nell Gwyn: Dorothy Gish in the title role

he didn't. He gave you the basis of the idea, and if you were over-doing it, he'd say, 'Too much—don't do so much. Be, don't act. Be it.' You didn't want to get caught acting. You wanted to persuade people, whatever it was, that this was happening and this was real."

One can't help wondering if Lillian didn't regret that she had pushed so much to have Dorothy in the film. For *Hearts of the World* is entirely Dorothy's picture. She is utterly delightful as the street singer trying to make herself as attractive as possible to Robert Harron with "perseverance and perfume," and shrugging her shoulders when she realises Harron's love belongs elsewhere, secure in her philosophy, "If you can't get what you want, want what you can get."

For the film, Dorothy wore a black wig, which led to some amusing incidents later, as people failed to recognize her as the girl in the film. Dorothy told Adela Rogers St. Johns, "There was a woman sat next to mother and me one day at a matinee of *Hearts of the World*. The woman watched me on the screen for a few minutes and then she turned around to me and said, 'I'll bet that girl is a tough one. She couldn't pull that stuff so well if she wasn't.'" (47)

As a result of her performance in *Hearts of the World,* Dorothy was offered a million-dollar contract by Paramount-Artcraft. She turned it down, preferring to remain with Griffith, an instance of the loyalty which crops up time and time again in recounting the careers of the Griffith actresses. After her decision to stay, Griffith supervised a series of seven Paramount-Artcraft comedies, directed by Elmer Clifton and starring Dorothy. These comedies, in fact, were so successful and popular that they helped to pay the cost of the building of Griffith's new studios at Mamaroneck.

They were equally popular with the critics, as the following reviews from *Wid's Film Daily* testify. *I'll Get Him Yet* (reviewed May 25, 1919): "Dorothy Gish has scored again. Individuality is marked in almost everything she does and the merest suggestion of a comic incident is frequently turned into a full-fledged laugh owing to her skill." *Nugget Nell* (reviewed August 3, 1919): "She knew just where to draw the line between seriousness and burlesque, with the result that time and time again she put a situation over with a bang. She was particularly bright in scoring in little things—the sort of things that made her efforts in the comedy line bring laughs merely because of her manner of doing them, and not always because of any inherent humor in the things themselves."

Late in 1919, Lillian began work on her first and only film as a director, *Remodelling Her Husband*. As her stars she had Dorothy and James Rennie, whom Dorothy was to marry on December 20, 1920. "Griffith needed money as usual," recalled Lillian, "and he wanted to go to Florida with his company and make the exteriors down there for two pictures quickly. And he said, 'How would you like to direct a picture with your sister? I don't want to break up a happy family, but I think you could do it. I think you know as much

Nell Gwyn: Gibb McLaughlin looks on disapprovingly as the King (Randle Ayrton) favors Nell with his attention

Madame Pompadour: Dorothy Gish in the title role of her last silent film

about movies as I do.' Well, I went home, and talked it over with mother and Dorothy to see if they thought it was a good idea. Of course, there was no story. Dorothy thought it was all right, and we got a little piece of business Dorothy found out of a funny magazine, and wrote a whole story around that. I asked if I could have Dorothy Parker* come and help me with the subtitles, because she'd never written for films, but I thought she was so witty and so bright— and I wanted it to be an all-woman picture too! Then Griffith left with everybody. He left Harry Carr—he was a brilliant man, the *Los Angeles Times* editorial writer—and me to do this film. I was taking scenes—it was December—and I'd have Dorothy and James Rennie playing the love scene, and it looked as if they were blowing smoke in one another's faces, it was so cold. I had to go down to New Rochelle quickly and get all my scenery; I had to design all the scenery, there were no set designers. Dorothy helped with her costumes, but I had to see to all the furniture, everything. George Hill was the cameraman, and he had had shell shock and was hysterical. And I know I got my main set, the living room, so big and not high enough at the back, so that if he took the whole room in, he shot over the top. And he threw his hat in the air, stamped on it, and had hysterics about that. I had to keep him calm. And then I had to build the studio!

"When I moved down there, I had to see the furnace was put in, and that the heat was sufficient. I had only fifty thousand dollars to make this picture with. We had a scene of Fifth Avenue, and the day before we took it, I found you had to have a police permit, and if that happened, I had all my crew on salary over the Christmas holidays. I said, 'I just can't. It's too far over the budget.' And I asked the crew and company if they would take a chance of going to jail with me, because we were doing something illegal.

"Well, 57th Street and Fifth Avenue is the busiest section in New York, and I had to have a bus go by a taxi cab, the wife sitting on top of the bus seeing her husband with a woman in the taxi cab. And we had no permit! We had the cameras in the car ahead, and as we turned a policeman saw what was happening, and held up his hand. Then he looked up at me, and he looked again, and then he put his fingers to his mouth and forced a smile. I said, 'Yes.' He waved us on, and we got by. We finished fifty-eight thousand dollars, and it made, I think, ten times what it cost, which not many pictures do today.

*The film does not credit Dorothy Parker.

London (1927): Dorothy Gish reunited with her old adversary, Gibb Mc-
Laughlin

"When Griffith came back, I asked him why he did that to me, had
me get a studio ready and make a picture, when it was the first one
and such an awful chore. He said, 'Because I needed my studio built
quickly, and I knew they'd work faster for a girl than they would
for me. I'm no fool.' And his studio was ready when he came back;
he moved right in."

Centennial Summer (1946): Dorothy Gish and Linda Darnell

After three pictures with other directors, Dorothy returned to Griffith, to appear with Lillian in what was to prove the sisters' final film for the great director, *Orphans of the Storm*. Griffith must have surprised many of his contemporaries by casting Dorothy not as Henriette, the more forceful of the two sisters, but as Louise, the blind girl, who is separated from her sister upon arrival in Paris, where they have come to find a surgeon who could cure the girl's blindness. Yet again, Dorothy proved that she was far more than the comedienne many people remember. It is hard to believe that Lillian could have put more emotion into the scenes in which Dorothy is forced by Lucille La Verne to sing and beg for money in the streets. "This production is so colossal in conception and in execution; its great moments move one so much; its thrills are so stirring, it is difficult to pin it to paper," commented *Photoplay*. "As for the acting—it is superb."

In the next four years, Dorothy appeared in only seven productions, two of which, *The Bright Shawl* (1923) and *Romola* (1924), have become classics, classics which, unhappily, it is impossible to view today. *Romola* was shot by Henry King in Italy, and Harry Carr reported in *Motion Picture Magazine* on the return of the two sisters to Hollywood for the premiere of the film. "The Gish sisters came out on the stage together when the picture was over, and Lillian made a frightened but sincere little speech. They were dressed in quaint, lovely gowns that somehow gave the impression that they were not quite of this world. Out there, behind the footlights, they looked like two fragile and beautiful little flowers."

Then, in 1926, Dorothy was invited to England by Herbert Wilcox to play the title role in *Nell Gwyn*. Dorothy gladly accepted, and came over to London with her husband, who appeared on the English stage in *The Great Gatsby*. (So impressed, in fact, by James Rennie was Wilcox—he described him to me as "a damned good actor"— that Rennie was given a role in Wilcox's 1933 production of *The Little Damozel*.)

Dorothy was joined in the film by some of the best acting talent that England had to offer at that time, including Randle Ayrton as the king, and Sydney Fairbrother as her mother. The film was an instantaneous success, and may well be the best picture Dorothy ever made. As critic George Jean Nathan commented, "It took a British director and an English-made film to reveal how sexy Dorothy Gish can be." And "sexy" indeed she is, displaying much of her very beautiful body, and obviously enjoying every minute of her seduction by the king. No wonder *Photoplay* pointed out, "Just for the grown-ups."

Nell Gwyn has been revived in recent years, thanks to George Eastman House, and has delighted new generations of filmgoers. Blanche Sweet saw the film again at a three-day tribute to Dorothy at the Museum of Modern Art, and told me, "Really in *Nell Gwyn* she was so lovely, so funny and so good. It was just a pleasure to see the picture again. It hadn't deteriorated; it was just as good as it always has been."

Dorothy made four more films for Herbert Wilcox: *London, Tip Toes,* and *Madame Pompadour,* all released in 1927, and *Wolves,* which was released in 1930, and which Wilcox claims as the first English all-talkie. Only *Madame Pompadour* appears to have survived from this group, and I was able to arrange for its first screening in forty years at London's National Film Theatre in the spring of 1971. The film proved to be a bitter disappointment. Dorothy's acting was faultless, as was that of her leading man, Antonio Moreno, and that of the villainous Gibb McLaughlin, but they were no match for a weak story and direction which seems antiquated and without the brilliance one would expect from the man responsible for *Nell Gwyn.*

Like her sister, Dorothy returned to the stage with the coming of sound. Her theater work included *Autumn Crocus* (1932), *Life with Father* (1939), *The Great Big Doorstep* (1942), and *The Magnificent Yankee* (1946). Dorothy made her American talkie debut in 1944, as the wife of Otis Skinner in the charming *Our Hearts Were Young and Gay.* She made only three more films: *Centennial Summer* (1946), *The Whistle at Eaton Falls* (1951), and *The Cardinal* (1964).

Dorothy Gish died of a stroke at a sanatorium in Rapallo, Italy, on June 4, 1968. Lillian was at the bedside. Lillian had written of her sister in *Theatre Magazine* (November 1927), "She is laughter, even on the cloudy days of life; nothing bothers her or saddens her or concerns her lastingly. Trouble gives only an evanescent shadow to her eyes and is banished with the shrug of a shoulder. I envy this dear, darling Dorothy with all my heart, for she is the side of me that God left out." That is how many, many filmgoers will remember Dorothy—as laughter.

6
Lillian Gish

Like she really comes on like a star.
It's really too much; she gassed me.
I think I love her.
—Student at Toronto's York University

In August of 1925, *Motion Picture Magazine* carried a photograph of Lillian and Dorothy Gish with their mother, which was captioned "The Proudest Little Mother in All the World." One can well appreciate that title for Mrs. Gish, mother of two great film actresses, one of whom, Lillian, has become one of the cinema's most endearing and enduring stars.

Lillian Gish must surely be the only film actress from the silent era to have become a legend in her own lifetime. It seems totally inexcusable to criticize anything that she may have said or done. As one reviewer, writing of her autobiography, pointed out, to criticize Lillian Gish is comparable to denying God, one's mother, and one's country in the same breath. Since that fateful day when she and her sister Dorothy were first introduced to Mr. Griffith at the Biograph studios, the legendary image of Lillian Gish has been growing. She might almost be said to have been nurturing that image from her birth in Springfield, Ohio, on October 14, 1896.

Writers today idolize her. Edward Wagenknecht has been one of

Lillian Gish

her sincerely devoted admirers for probably longer than most people. In 1927 he wrote, "She is completely a being of lyric loveliness, even to her very name." (55) Sewell Stokes, in a radio broadcast in January, 1958, commented, "My favourite heroine was a wistful girl with a rosebud mouth and large dreamy eyes. She was beautiful and had about her a frail, spiritual quality that set her apart from the others. From my earliest visits to the cinema I had been in love with her. I had worshiped her from afar; she was a goddess, set on a very high pedestal indeed. And her name was Lillian Gish."

Of course, during the silent era itself, Miss Gish was not quite as revered as she is today. Marion Davies in *The Patsy* gives a brilliantly cruel parody of a Lillian Gish portrayal. James R. Quirk wrote in *Photoplay,* "In the last twelve years she has been saved just in the nick of time from the brutal attacks of 4,000 German soldiers, 2,000 border ruffians, and 999 conscienceless men about town. Someday I hope the American hero breaks a leg and fails to get there before the German soldier smashes in the door." (39) The editor of another contemporary film magazine commented, "An optimist is a person who will go to the theater expecting to see a D. W. Griffith production in which Lillian Gish is not attacked by the villain in the fifth reel." One newspaper critic even suggested the foundation of a Society for the Prevention of Cruelty to Lillian Gish.

Lillian Gish and David Wark Griffith; the two names are synonymous. Lillian Gish has starred in more Griffith features than any other actress, and she has carried on the acting tradition that Griffith taught her into the present. She was the ethereal star, who to most people represented the D. W. Griffith school of acting, the helpless heroine menaced by the villainous thug, be it in *The Birth of a Nation, Hearts of the World,* or *Broken Blossoms.* Lillian Gish was—and is—the supreme Griffith actress.

Of her films at American Biograph, I feel *The Mothering Heart,* released on June 21, 1913, was probably Lillian's best work. It contains the typical Griffith-Gish traits—the death of the baby, the vamp who lures the husband away—but it also contains a superb, adult performance from Miss Gish. Lillian has discovered her husband's (Walter Miller) unfaithfulness by finding a glove belonging to the other woman (Viola Barry*) in his jacket pocket. She leaves him and goes to her mother (Kate Bruce). After the death of their baby, Miller returns. Lillian finds him by the baby's cot and tells him to go, but then she sees that he has the child's pacifier in his hand, and realizes her continuing love for him. The film contains some surpris-

---

* Viola Barry was one of the silent cinema's most believable vamps. The daughter of the socialist politician, J. Stitt Wilson, she was married to director Jack Conway, whom she met in 1911 while he was an actor with the Bison Company and she was working with the Burbank Stock Company.

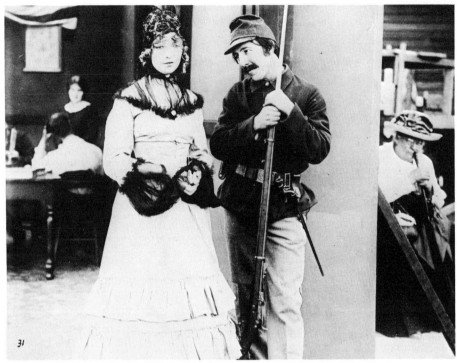

The Birth of a Nation: Lillian Gish with the "mooning sentry" (William Freeman)

Lillian Gish in *True Heart Susie*

Hearts of the World: Lillian Gish and Noel Coward

ingly mature acting from Lillian (bearing in mind her age at this time), particularly a long, hard look directly into the camera after the death of her child, and a scene of savage, silent fury as she relieves all her pent-up emotions by beating a bush—each stroke a blow against those who have wronged her by taking away both her husband and her child.

No one will ever know whether Griffith was aware then of the actress, the star, he had in Lillian Gish. Certainly, he took Lillian with him when he moved on to Reliance-Majestic, but he did not in any way favor her. He was obviously aware of her ethereal qualities when he cast her as John Howard Payne's sweetheart in *Home Sweet Home*. It is to Lillian that Henry B. Walthall, as Payne, says "Till the end of the world and afterwards I shall wait for you," which brings Lillian's reply, "It will be happiness to wait for him."

Writing of that period in *Harper's Bazaar*, Lillian recalled the lesson that Griffith always drilled into his actresses: "Griffith always told us there was no quick or easy way to stardom, and that being a star had nothing to do with having your name in the papers or up in lights over the marquees of theaters. You were a star only when you

Lillian Gish in *Broken Blossoms*

had won your way into the hearts of people. He claimed that this
would take at least ten years, that we must make pictures so good
that they would be worthy of the effort sometimes necessary to see
them." (23)

It was not until *The Birth of a Nation* and Lillian's role as Elsie

Way Down East: Lillian Gish and Lowell Sherman

Stoneman that the world really sat up and took notice. Lillian recalled for me that Blanche Sweet was originally slated for the part. "She was really, I think, to have had this part in *The Birth of a Nation*, but I rehearsed for her. If they were making another film, which no doubt she'd be doing with some other director, Griffith would want to rehearse *The Birth,* and whoever was free would rehearse any part, men and women. And one time I was rehearsing, and George Sieg-mann was playing the mulatto, and in my excitement at trying to be good and impress Mr. Griffith my hair came down—long, blonde hair to below my waist. I was very thin and unformed, and he picked me up, and my hair and feet almost touched the floor on both sides of him. And Griffith thought, well maybe he saw a full mature figure as Elsie Stoneman, maybe a frail figure with the hair and all would be more effective. I think that's how I got the job. I didn't think I was to play Elsie Stoneman; I wasn't that far up in the company at that time. It was by rights Blanche Sweet's part."

After *The Birth* came Griffith's greatest work, *Intolerance.* So much has—rightly—been written about this production that there seems little to add here. As Lillian commented, "The man had it all in his mind. He wrote every bit of it, he designed every set, he de-signed every costume, it was all his. That's his monument. It is the greatest film ever made." Lillian wrote in a letter to the widow of Howard Gaye, who portrayed The Christ in the film, "When Dorothy and I went to Jerusalem two years ago we felt it had been built by Mr. Griffith, and we expected to see your dear husband coming down the street any moment."

The series of Griffith productions that followed *Intolerance* served further to assert Lillian's position as the silent screen's greatest dra-matic actress, to make her, in the words of Harry Carr, "the supreme technician of the screen."

It is unfair to single out any individual film, but if I had to, then I would say *Broken Blossoms,* closely followed by *True Heart Susie,* was her finest achievement. Julian Johnson wrote of the former in *Photoplay* (August, 1919), "It is the finest genuine tragedy of the movies. The visualizing of this bitter-sweet story is, I have no hesi-tation in saying, the very finest expression of the screen so far. There seems to be no setting or accessory which is not correct in its finest details. The composition is a painter's. The photography is not only perfect, but, with caution, is innovational, and approximates, in its larger lights and softnesses of close view, the details of bright and dark upon the finest canvases in the Louvres of the world."

Lillian Gish as the London waif beaten by a drunken father and idolized by the love-sick Chinaman is beauty personified. Every sub-title is almost a poem to her loveliness: "He breathed into an amber flute the alabaster cockney girl's love name—White Blossom" or "There he brings rays stolen from the lyric moon and places them in

The White Sister: Lillian Gish and Ronald Colman

her hair, and all night long he holds her grubby hand." Through Lillian Gish's portrayal, the spirit of beauty truly has broken her blossoms about our chambers. Julian Johnson, in his *Photoplay* review, said of her, "She has to be both Lillian Gish and the Mae Marsh

La Boheme: Lillian Gish and John Gilbert

of old rolled into one sorrowful little being, and her success in this strange combination of motives and beings is absolute."

The closet scene, with Lillian whirling around and around in terror, is one of the most famous moments in silent film drama, as is the gesture of Lillian forcing her mouth into a smile with her fingers. "I know I was rehearsing the child in *The Chink and the Child,* that was called *Broken Blossoms* you know, and in rehearsal I just put the smile on my face. I hadn't thought of it, but it just happened. And he [Griffith] jumped up, and he said, 'Where did you get that gesture? How did you think of that? I've never seen that—that's the most original gesture we've had in the movie.' And he then immediately put it all through the film. He grabs something quickly that he felt was good, and enlarges upon it and uses it."

True Heart Susie was released prior to *Broken Blossoms* on June 1, 1919. Lillian portrays Susie, a country girl whose love for a local boy, Robert Harron, is responsible for her paying for him to go through college, enter the ministry, and, unexpectedly, marry another woman. The Gish characterization is not as easy to analyze as many people would believe. She is not the simple country girl of the written synopsis. *Wid's Film Daily's* summing up of her philosophy is true enough: "Her philosophy of life is so simple and beautiful. She loves, and to her love means sacrifice and an abiding faith in the ultimate goodness of things." But the Gish characterization hints not so much at a selfless sacrifice, but at a sacrifice for a purpose, a sacrifice that eventually will bring her the man she loves. When that sacrifice does not work out exactly as she had planned, and the man she loves marries another woman, then her spite may not be openly visible, but it is there nevertheless, only just beneath the surface. Watch Lillian's eyes in *True Heart Susie*. They are not the eyes of a selfless, simple girl. They are the eyes of a devoted creature, until Harron meets Clarine Seymour, and then those eyes are filled with spite and hatred. You know Lillian will get her man, no matter how long she may have to wait.

At the time of its original release, *True Heart Susie* was not particularly well-received. *Wid's Film Daily* (June 8, 1919) thought, "The trouble here is that there is not enough plot substance to balance properly a production of this length. At times the picture drags, not through any deficiencies on the part of the players, or any shortcomings in the direction, rather owing to a lack of variety in the action. The thinness of the plot makes necessary the too frequent repetition of scenes that in their meaning and expression of emotion are virtually the same. In more abbreviated form, *True Heart Susie* might easily have become a masterpiece of screen character fiction. At present it suggests an ideal short story expanded to novel length."

In the twenties, Lillian made only two Griffith films, *Way Down East* and *Orphans of the Storm*. Then Griffith allowed her to go her own way. Today, that hardly seems believable. How could a director

Lillian Gish fights a losing battle in, and against, *The Wind*

bear to lose an actress of whom *Photoplay*, reviewing *Orphans of the Storm*, had written, "Each new Gish portrayal is finer than the one before. The actress *works*. With a rare beauty and personal charm, she is not content. Her Henriette is sublime." Happily, Lillian Gish did not seem in any way to be lost without Griffith's guiding hand. Indeed, many would say it was the director who suffered the loss.

Lillian carried the techniques that she had learned under Griffith into the films of other directors, beginning with *The White Sister*, premiered on September 5, 1923 at New York's 44th Street Theater. Lillian was—and still is—devoted to *The White Sister* and its theme.

"Richard Barthelmess had left us after *Way Down East*, and then he came back. Under his arm he had *Tol'able David*, and he ran it for us in the projection room one night. Well, we all wept, and Griffith wept, and we were so happy. Griffith hugged and kissed him and said, with the tears in his eyes, how proud he was of him, because he just loved his children to go out and make a success of their own. Then Dick said, why didn't I come with Inspiration. Well, I found *The White Sister*, and worked on the script because I wanted it for a new

Lillian Gish, Constance Collier, and Mary Pickford attend a 1939 Hollywood premiere

scene that had never been seen on films—and that was the taking of the veil. And I somehow got hold of the ritual, which was a beautiful and sensuous poem. I'm not a Catholic, but I thought it was so dramatic to say 'the bridegroom' and flash to the crucifix. Henry

King didn't think much of the story, but he would have made the telephone book to get to Italy. It was just a sensational success. It was the first modern religious film ever made. Up until then, they had made Biblical stories, but this was the first modern religious film."

Unhappily, aside from Lillian's performance, the film does not stand up too well today. The direction lacks polish, and there is no excuse for Henry King shooting in the day for night shots, so that the sunlight is clearly visible streaming through the trees.

But it is to Lillian that one looks, and she does not let one down. Who else but Lillian Gish could have been the "ethereal child" of F. Marion Crawford's novel? As *Photoplay* noted, "Her work is more evenly balanced and human. She is a woman, rather than a temperamentally high-strung girl." The scenes in which Lillian takes the veil must be, as she has rightly pointed out, some of the most beautiful ever filmed. "Today you are at liberty to go into the world— tomorrow the doors will be closed forever," says the Mother Superior to Lillian before the ceremony begins. "Clothed in bridal array for her marriage to the church," the girl goes before the altar. Three old nuns watch her; the spectator knows that they are remembering the vows that they took so many years ago. As the ceremony progresses, there are only three titles: "Wedding Bells," "The Bride," and finally, with a cut to the figure of Christ on the cross above the altar, "The Bridegroom." Lillian's hair is cut. She is now the "spouse of Christ."

Lillian was not particularly happy, one suspects, working with Henry King, but for the majority of her other productions in the 1920s she chose her directors carefully. "Oh, I was so happy working with Mr. Seastrom and that great Swedish actor Lars Hanson— beautiful artists. I'd been away from Hollywood so long, I didn't know the directors or actors, and I saw just two reels of an unfinished film called *The Big Parade*. And I said I'd like to have that director and those actors for my first film [at MGM], and they gave all of them to me. I don't think they realised what a wonderful film at that time *The Big Parade* was, but I could tell in a rough cut this was something unusual and fine."

King Vidor's autobiography, *A Tree Is a Tree,* makes it obvious that the director had great respect for Miss Gish. Their mutual respect was undoubtedly responsible for making *La Boheme* the fine production that it is—although it was not the success it should have been.

La Boheme was taken from the same source as Puccini's opera,

Follow Me, Boys: Lillian Gish as Hetty Seiber (courtesy of Walt Disney Productions)

Henri Murger's *Life in the Latin Quarter*. Lillian is introduced as an embroideress, first seen sewing in the cold of her tiny, bare room, "facing life with a glorious courage." The film contains perhaps the most harrowing of Gish sequences, certainly as disturbing as the final rescue from the ice floe in *Way Down East;* this is Mimi's dying flight through the cobbled streets of Montmartre, roaming, it almost

Follow Me, Boys: Elliott Reid, Lillian Gish, Fred MacMurray, and Vera Miles (courtesy of Walt Disney Productions)

seems, endlessly through the streets, holding on to passing carriages. The film also contains a number of attempts by Lillian at comedy: shielding her eyes and crossing herself as John Gilbert crosses the roof from his apartment to her room, acting out an entire play—including a duel—for the Count, and looking through opera glasses from the wrong end.

Lillian did not work again with King Vidor until 1946 when she appeared as Mrs. McCanles in David Selznick's production of *Duel in the Sun*. Lillian is one of the completely "good" people in the story; Jennifer Jones, in fact, says to her, "I'll be a good girl—I want to be like you." And it was this type of role that Lillian was to play in all of her sound pictures. One of the reasons why she has devoted herself more to the stage and less to the cinema since the coming of sound may very well have been the lack of variety in the parts that she has been offered.

To my mind at least, her most pleasing performance in recent years, and one which carries on very much the tradition established by D. W. Griffith, was that of Hetty Seiber in Walt Disney's *Follow Me Boys*, released in 1966.

The first time that Jennifer Jones, as Pearl Chavez, meets Lillian in *Duel in the Sun,* the elder lady talks of Jennifer Jones's father, saying "I'm somewhat different than he remembered." That statement cannot be applied to the actual Lillian Gish. For more than fifty years, she has remained one of the few stable things in the film industry. A Lillian Gish performance, one always knows, will be a good performance, whether it be in a film, in her autobiography, or in her stage presentation of *Lillian Gish and the Movies.*

At the end of her delightful autobiography, in writing of D. W. Griffith, Lillian makes her own evaluation of her life. "It seems to me that a happy life should be in balance, that one must live equally in the mind, body and spirit. I carry with me one of D. W.'s favorite quotations. 'What you get is living. What you give is life.'" (24)

7

Mae Marsh

She was the only actress
of whom I was ever jealous.
—Lillian Gish (24)

Of all the actresses who appeared in Griffith's productions, Mae Marsh is the one whom Griffith most successfully molded into the characters he wished her to play. Without him she never seemed able to give of her best, but under his direction she gave some of the silent screen's greatest performances. Indeed, as Iris Barry has said, in *Intolerance* she gave a performance and a characterization unequalled by any silent player.

Much of Griffith's success with her was probably due to Mae's innocence and naïveté, a naïveté which remained with her all her life, as her few writings and interviews prove. Her devotion to Griffith was absolute. In 1948 she wrote: "Mr. Griffith was always solicitous about what we called *The Birth of a Nation* family, proud when many of us went on to individual successes, sad when others were beset by misfortune." (40) In a letter to a fan, written in 1936, she said, "Mr. Griffith was a wonderful teacher; he had a great understanding of all life; the kittens he used in *The Birth* acted to his instructions as well as his people and the same was with every picture. I only wish we had someone today to train our young ambitious people."

Mae Marsh

Even though Griffith let her go, just as he let all of his greatest discoveries go, the director was obviously very fond of Mae. In an article in the *Chicago Illinstrated World* (October, 1921) he wrote, "I have found that if actors do not have sweetness inside them, you cannot get it into a photograph of them. No man on earth can bring out what isn't there. And I say this strictly, I think, in illustration of little Mae Marsh, whom the critics have compared with Duse, even, and Sarah Bernhardt, and mentioned what one of them described as 'a kind of aura before her face.' On the screen she is always beautiful, and in life as well. She is a wonderful little girl who isn't strong at all, yet she takes care of her mother and is sending her sisters to school. She supports her family." In 1923, Griffith told *Photoplay*'s Delight Evans, "Every other motion picture star I have known was 'made' by long training and much hard work, but Mae Marsh was born a film star. Destiny itself seemed to have been her coach in acting."

Mary Warne Marsh was born on November 9, 1895 in Madrid, New Mexico, where her father, who traveled as an auditor for the Santa Fe Railroad, and her mother happened to be at the time. Mae's oldest sister, Marguerite, had become an actress in New York, and when she rejoined her family in Los Angeles, she entered films.

As Mae also wanted to become an actress, she persuaded her sister to take her along one day to the studios. According to Mae, it was January 8, 1912 when she first entered Biograph's West Coast studios. In 1918, she reminisced to Hazel Simpson Naylor of *Motion Picture Classic,* "I was taken into the studio and introduced to Mary Pickford. I remember thinking to myself, 'Humph! She isn't so much, just kinda fat and all curls! But Blanche Sweet—Blanche Sweet was the idol of my heart in those days. No one, to my mind, could be half so great, and when she flounced in wearing a tight dress, a huge black hat and a veil, I was so thrilled I choked right up to here. They pretty much ignored me, to tell the truth."

But Griffith did not ignore her; according to Linda Arvidson, he told her, "I'll remember, and I'll put you in a movie some day." (1) That first movie was probably *A Siren of Impulse,* released March 12, 1912. The director also changed her name from Mary to Mae, thinking that one Mary in the company was more than enough.

Mae's first starring role came with *Man's Genesis,* released July 11, 1912. How she came to get that part has often been told, but as Blanche Sweet comments, "That's a story that's been wrongly done, not that it makes the slightest difference; the story was funny enough, but it's funnier in two ways. I was approached—not approached— told to do it. I was going to do it, and for some reason I refused to do it, and I don't know why. It is said I wouldn't wear a grass skirt with bare legs. Well, the grass skirt was about the size of a barrel, and went way down. And I had danced with Gertrude Hoffman on the stage in a little wisp of chiffon that went nowhere at all, and had

Mae Marsh as "The Little Sister" of *The Birth of a Nation*

never thought anything about it. So why I wouldn't wear a grass skirt when I'd danced in chiffon I'll never know. But I was given to being that way in my younger days. That was just unheard of, and it was an awful pall that fell over the studio, and nobody spoke to me—they were afraid to. Then he told Mary to do it, and she said, 'No.' And

Mae Marsh and Robert Harron in *Intolerance*: "Their First Meeting"

then, of course, he gave it to Mae, and it didn't mean anything to her. It shouldn't have meant anything to any of us.

"Then came *The Sands of Dee*, which both Mary and I wanted and thought we should have, either one of us, and he gave it to Mae.

Intolerance: Mae Marsh and "the hopeful geranium"

That aroused all sorts of resentment on our part. Then came the time for us to go back to New York, and by that time I was pretty mad about everything. So we were stopping off at Albuquerque on the way back and doing a rather large Indian picture with Mary.* I went to Griffith and said, 'I'm not in this picture, so I would like to be allowed to go back to New York with my grandmother. There's no sense in my sitting around a week or two in Albuquerque.' Very grimly he said, 'You are not allowed to go back to New York; you'll go to Albuquerque and stay there.' So there was no arguing that point! It was very hot in Albuquerque, of course, and they came back just dead tired, hot and disagreeable—you know, in the desert, sand in your mouth, blowing up your nose, and in your food. And I made a point of having a shower just before they came back, and sitting in a nice cool dress, and I had a sherry cobbler with lots of ice and some fruit in it. I made a point to sit there every day when they came back from location, not for them, but for Griffith because he wouldn't let me go back to New York. That's why I say I'm sure that's how it

* *A Pueblo Romance,* released August 29, 1912.

happened. I was punished. Nobody else was punished for refusing to play a film. I was the one that was punished."

Mae Marsh remained in California when Griffith and the company returned to New York, but when Mary Pickford told him that she intended leaving the company, the director remembered her and wired her to come to New York and join the company on a permanent basis. In the meantime, Mae had appeared in two productions for the Kalem Company, but she was far from happy with that company or her director there, Kenean Buell.

Mae was an obvious choice for Griffith to take with him to Reliance-Majestic, where she appeared in, among other things, *The Escape, Home Sweet Home,* and *The Avenging Conscience,* all released in 1914. Her finest performance at this time was probably in *Home Sweet Home,* in which she appeared as "Apple Pie Mary," betrothed to Robert Harron, "a fortune-seeking youth from the East." One of the most touching sequences in the film is Harron's departure, when he, having nothing else to give her in remembrance, leaves his spectacles, and Mae in return says, "I got no picture to give you but this Christmas card looks like me." When Harron later hears the fateful song, "Home Sweet Home," and returns to Mae, he finds her hiding under the bed, wearing his spectacles. By this time the partnership of Robert Harron and Mae Marsh had become firmly established, and it is tragic that Mae's eventual departure from the Griffith company and Harron's tragic death prevented their continuing the partnership into the twenties.

To generations of filmgoers, Mae will always be remembered as Flora, "the little sister" of *The Birth of a Nation.* Indeed, at the time of her death, *Classic Film Collector* ran a full-page obituary, headed "Farewell—Little Sister." Who can forget Mae's hysterical laughter as she and the other womenfolk of the Cameron family hide in the cellar as the house is invaded by renegade soldiers, or the moment that she shyly welcomes home Henry B. Walthall, and then breaks the tension by pointing to a bullet hole in his hat. One of Mae's most devoted admirers, film historian Harold Dunham, has written, "I was quite young when I first saw Mae on the screen—she came out from her Southern home, with her elder sister Miriam Cooper, and was wearing, as I recall it, a pretty short-sleeved gingham dress, and carrying a little parasol—and I immediately fell in love with her. When later she died in her brother's arms at the foot of a high rock, I felt that the light had gone from the film. The fact that I should not see this charming creature again tore at my heart. I have never

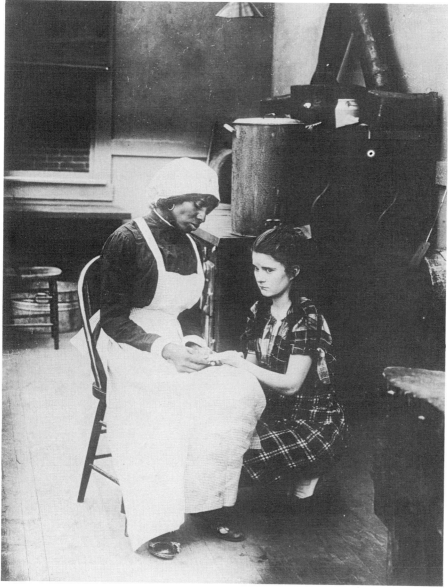

Hoodoo Ann (1916): Mae Marsh and Madame Sul-Te-Wan

seen *The Birth of a Nation* since without experiencing something of the same feeling." (20)

The critics went wild over her playing. Alexander Woollcott described her as "the most exquisitely sensitive face the screen has found." Warde Greene in *The Atlanta Journal* commented, "That

Paddy-the-Next-Best-Thing: Mae Marsh and George K. Arthur

little sister—she is wonderful. Mae Marsh is the girl who plays the role, plays it with an abandon and sincerity that is not acting but living. There, at last, when she goes to the dark spring for water, you see her smiling gayly at a squirrel on a limb; you see the bright-eyed animal swallow a nut. You follow her mad race through the woods from the black crazed by power. You are with her when she pauses on the precipice and when she plunges downward and rolls over and over at the bottom to writhe for a moment, crushed and broken, before her head snaps back." And in one sentence, the *New York Dramatic Mirror* summed it all up: "Mae Marsh surpasses the fondest prophecies of her admirers."

With her next role, as the girl of the modern story of *Intolerance,* Mae did the impossible—she surpassed her performance in *The Birth of a Nation,* and gave the silent cinema its greatest acting moments. The scene in the courtroom will live forever, for, as Pauline Kael wrote in *The New Yorker,* "The girl who twists her hands in the courtroom scenes of *Intolerance* is the image of youth in trouble forevermore." Mae has always disclaimed any credit for her performance —it was all Griffith. "I have seen *Intolerance* twenty times, I suppose," she said in 1917, "and it never occurs to me that 'the girl' in the modern episode is myself. It is all Mr. Griffith. When I watch her actions I am no more able to disassociate Mr. Griffith from them than I am able to watch the Babylonian spectacles without thinking of him. In his pictures everything—scenery and players—is just so many instruments in his orchestra." (4)

In her delightful semiautobiographical *Screen Acting,* published in 1921, she wrote: "The hardest dramatic work I ever did was in the courtroom scenes in *Intolerance.* We retook these scenes on four different occasions. Each time I gave to the limit of my vitality and ability. I put everything into my portrayal that was in me. It certainly paid. Parts of each of the four takes—some of them done at two weeks' intervals—were assembled to make up those scenes which you, as the audience, finally beheld upon the screen." (33)

After the completion of *Intolerance,* Mae was starred in a series of delightful productions for release by Triangle. All were supervised by Griffith, but they were directed by others, including Lloyd Ingraham (*Hoodoo Ann, The Little Liar*), Paul Powell (*The Wild Girl of the Sierras*) and Chester Withy (*The Wharf Rat*).

Then, in 1917, Mae was approached by the Goldwyn Company and offered $2,500 a week to sign an exclusive contract. Like others before her, she went to tell Griffith, expecting him to ask her to stay, but he did not. Griffith told her to go and earn the money that she deserved. It was a bad move. Mae was unhappy with the Goldwyn Company, and her films made there were poorly received. "Where is Mae Marsh?" screamed *Photoplay.* "Hasn't the real Mae Marsh, the wide-eyed little mistress of pathos that we used to know, been gone from the screen a long time?" Mae herself pleaded, "I want

The White Rose: Ivor Novello asks Mae Marsh for her forgiveness as Carol Dempster and Lucille La Verne look on.

The Rat: Ivor Novello and Mae Marsh

Over the Hill: Mae Marsh, James Kirkwood and Tommy Conlon

Over the Hill: Mae Marsh, Sally Eilers, James Kirkwood, and James Dunn

parts like 'Apple Pie Mary' in *Home Sweet Home,* or the gamin in *A Child of the Paris Streets,* or the boy in *The Wharf Rat.* These are real individuals—not just girls that someone wants to marry, or wants somebody else not to marry, and all that sort of rot." Of the films that Mae made for Goldwyn between 1917 and 1919, she claimed to like only *Polly of the Circus* (directed in 1917 by Charles T. Horan and Edwin L. Hollywood) and *The Cinderella Man* (directed, also in 1917, by George Loane Tucker). The years at Goldwyn also marked her last appearance opposite Robert Harron in John Noble's *Sunshine Alley* (1917).

In 1918, Mae married Louis Lee Arms, one of Goldwyn's publicity men. It was a happy and a lasting marriage. When her Goldwyn contract expired, Mae announced her screen retirement, but in 1920 she was persuaded to return to the screen by Robertson-Cole, for whom she starred in John Adolfi's *The Little 'Fraid Lady.*

A number of films followed, usually for minor companies, the most charming of which is Howard Hickman's *Nobody's Kid,* released by Robertson-Cole in 1921. However, more typical is an offering from Warners, *Daddies,* directed in 1924 by William A. Seiter. In the film, a very mild comedy which found amusement in the adoption of war orphans by a bachelor's club, Mae has little or nothing to do. Indeed, in the first half of the picture, Mae's sole contribution is two fainting fits, and in the latter half she is simply required to look pretty and wistful in one scene.

However, in England, director Graham Cutts and producer Herbert Wilcox had formed their own company in 1921, and were beginning to make a name for themselves. Both men admired D. W. Griffith, and when they had the opportunity of spending what in England was a considerable sum of money on production, they decided that part of the funds should be used to import a Griffith star. Mae Marsh was the obvious choice. Mae starred in two productions in 1922, *Flames of Passion* and *Paddy-the-Next-Best-Thing,* and she was paid a salary of between 750 and 1,000 pounds per week. Mae was adored by the English public, and was mobbed on her arrival in London. Recalls Herbert Wilcox, "There must have been thirty to forty thousand people at Waterloo Station to meet this little wisp of a girl." The films were moderately successful, both in England and America, but Mae was not happy with England—"It never stopped raining."

Griffith had not forgotten Mae, however. In 1921, after attending a revival of *The Birth of a Nation,* he had cabled her, "Just saw the greatest performance ever seen on any screen . . . that of the little sister played by Miss Mae Marsh." In 1923, amid the beautiful scenery of Louisiana, Griffith began work on *The White Rose,* starring Mae Marsh, supported by Ivor Novello, Carol Dempster, and Neil Hamilton. Three lengthy opening titles explained the scope of the film: "A story different in that the fallen man suffers as well as the woman—also of woman's *enduring love,* that no error, shame or sorrow can destroy. . . . It concerns a few human beings—no mobs or melodramatic action—just people swayed by circumstances and environment. . . . It depends for interest upon the development and reflux of characters. They fall, sometimes they rise, even as you and I. The interest they hold depends upon the reflection in the dim halls of your heart." In these titles, Griffith seems almost to be saying, "Don't expect too much from this picture." They are curiously sad, particularly in view of critical reaction such as *Photoplay*'s "This sort of stuff is a complete waste of the genius of the man."

Mae plays Bessie, an orphan—"I am a *First Class Orphan*—you see I had a mama and a papa both"—who becomes a waitress and in time a flapper, nicknamed "Teazie." A seemingly idyllic love affair

Reminiscing in the forties: Donald Crisp, Mae Marsh, and Lillian Gish

with Ivor Novello brings about an unwanted child. "All your tears will undo no wrong. All your grief bring back no yesterday." With the baby, Mae can find neither work nor shelter; she contemplates suicide, and as she does we see a close-up of her hands, hands that seven years earlier had thrilled us so in *Intolerance*. She is taken in by a kindly black woman, Lucille La Verne, and Novello rights his wrong by marrying her. "A little, worn, outcast girl lights the room like an altar lamp, with the terrible mystery of woman's unselfish love." The picture is entirely Mae's; Carol Dempster and the two leading men matter not at all.

As *Photoplay* (August, 1923) pointed out, "Here alone the production reaches its height. Mae Marsh has several moments when she comes close to silver screen greatness. We are not so sure but that she touches it." Mae confessed, "It's a Mae Marsh part, which means I play a poor kid who gets herself into a terrific emotional tangle. It's a great part. And I'm scared to death of it."

In 1925, Mae returned to England for what was to be her last silent film, *The Rat,* again directed by Graham Cutts, but with Sir Michael Balcon producing. Ivor Novello wrote *The Rat* as a film script while working on *The White Rose*. He showed it to Constance Collier, and she persuaded him to rewrite it as a stage play. This he did—it was his first play as author and as actor-manager—and it opened in Brighton on January 15, 1924, transferring to London's Prince of Wales Theatre in June of the same year.

Michael Balcon approached Novello as to the possibility of a film version, and production began early in 1925 at London's Islington studios. The film has its faults, particularly in the story line (romantic melodrama does seem rather dated today), but it is brilliantly directed by Cutts and photographed by Hal Young. The playing of the three principals, Ivor Novello, Mae Marsh, and Isabel Jeans, cannot be faulted, and the film deservedly was one of the most popular British films of the period. Mae Marsh could not have wished for a better film to end her silent career.

Mae Marsh decided to retire from the screen and occupy herself as a housewife and a mother, but in 1932 she was persuaded by the Fox Film Company to make a comeback as the mother in Henry King's *Over the Hill*. It was a role created by Mary Carr in the silent era, and Mae's playing—both as a young and as an old woman —more than did the part justice.

After that Mae settled down to a long career playing cameo roles in films, usually for Twentieth Century-Fox. She never sought to play leads, because she had difficulty learning lines, but preferred to work

Mae Marsh in John Ford's *Sergeant Rutledge*

for a handful of directors whom she admired, in particular John Ford and Andrew Stone. She made her last screen appearance in John Ford's *Two Rode Together* (1961). It was with Ford that Mae had gone to pay her last respects to D. W. Griffith prior to his funeral.

Chapter Eleven of her *Screen Acting* is subtitled, "Mr. Griffith and some of his methods of direction—what everyone associated with the screen owes to him." She wrote:

"I have planned all along to dedicate this chapter to Mr. David Wark Griffith, and now that I have arrived at it, I find that my pen is unequal to the task. No mere chapter, nor book, could undertake to tell Mr. Griffith's importance to motion pictures. The things that he has accomplished in the past ten years, invariably in the face of great odds, almost pass belief.

"For Mr. Griffith I have the strong and mixed feeling that the child has for its benefactor, or the student for a beloved preceptor. At an age now where I can more appreciate the many trials that he endured I look back fondly to those days when Mary Pickford, Blanche Sweet, Lillian and Dorothy Gish, Robert Harron, and myself were beginning our careers and at the same time founding what has come to be known as the Griffith school." (33)

Mae Marsh, the little sister, died at her Hermosa Beach home on February 13, 1968.

8

Miriam Cooper

Black liquid eyes that sparkle and
rove and now and then alight, temptingly,
but—alas—momentarily.
—*Motion Picture Magazine*

Two things strike the viewer watching Miriam Cooper's performances
in *The Birth of a Nation* and *Intolerance,* the modernity of her beauty
and her eyes. Did any other star from the teens have such eyes? Jet
black eyes that seemed to haunt every scene in which she appeared,
eyes that today, apparently, shine just as sharply. A syndicated news
feature on the star by Michael Kernan, which appeared in many
American newspapers and which reported on a recent visit to her,
specifically mentioned those "dark, marvelous eyes that look straight
at you."

Miriam Cooper was unlike her contemporary Griffith actresses in
that hers was not a delicate beauty. Her looks have not dated in the
way that many people would argue the beauty of Lillian Gish or Mae
Marsh has dated. In many ways, Miss Cooper was a star of the
wrong decade. She did not belong to the teens; she belonged more
to the era of Clara Bow and Louise Brooks.

Miriam, or Marian, Cooper was born in Baltimore, Maryland, on
November 7, 1894. She was educated in convents in Baltimore and

Miriam Cooper

later in New York, where she also attended the Art Students League
and the Cooper Union High School. She was introduced to the cele-
brated painter and photographer, Harrison Fisher, and he used her
as a model for several of his portraits.

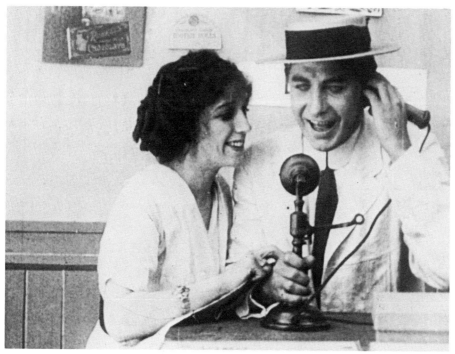

Miriam Cooper and Guy Coombs in Kalem's *A Railroad Lochinvar* (released September 14, 1912)

Her entry into films is shrouded in mystery. Contemporary magazine articles seem to indicate that she began her film career with the Kalem Company, but she has recently indicated that her film career began around 1910 with American Biograph. The following account of her entry into films appeared in *Reel Life* (June 13, 1914):

"One of the girls in the school suggested that she try motion pictures, and, fired with the flavor of adventure in the thing, Miss Cooper went to the Kalem office. She was accepted to work as an 'extra.' For two weeks she was kept busy nearly every day, and she earned twenty dollars. All the while she felt a guilty delight in her secret, for she knew her mother's opinion of anything connected with the stage or acting, and she dared not breathe a word about it at home for fear of being thwarted.

"But the movies would not so easily relinquish Miss Cooper. Not long after, the Kalem made her an offer to become a stock member of the company. She was too good an all-round athlete, too attractive a girl, and possessed of too pronounced dramatic ability for the movies to let her slip. Persuading her mother was the only hard part for

Miriam Cooper as the elder Cameron daughter in *The Birth of a Nation*

Miriam in getting into pictures. But at length, Mrs. Cooper reluctantly gave her consent. About two years ago, Miriam went to Florida with the Kalem Company, engaged by Kenean Buell to play ingenue parts. It was a matter of a few weeks before she was taking dramatic leads."

It is very difficult to discredit *Reel Life*'s straightforward account of Miriam's entry into films; it ties in with what she herself was to say in several interviews she gave prior to 1920, in many of which she credited Alice Joyce as being responsible for her film debut. Alice Joyce, apart from being Kalem's leading lady from 1912 onwards, was also a model, and it is highly probable that the two girls met at Harrison Fisher's studios.

If she did work for Griffith at American Biograph, then it was only for a very short period of time. And if she did, then why did the director let her go?

Miriam Cooper appeared in well over a hundred Kalem one- and two-reelers between 1912 and late 1913. They were mainly Civil War and railroad dramas, and Miriam played anything from leads to walk-ons. One of her Kalem releases, *The Battle of Bloody Ford,* released on March 22, 1913, received a very favorable review in *Moving Picture World:* "I think a special word of acknowledgment is due to Miss Marian [*sic*] Cooper, who took one of the principal parts. This young lady, though still in her teens, is a splendid athletic, a good runner, a graceful and skilled rider and a perfect swimmer. She gives most delightful exhibitions of her accomplishments. Withal she knows how to act and altogether is a distinct acquisition to the Kalem ranks."

In December, 1913, Griffith invited her to become a member of the Reliance stock company. Why Griffith should have chosen her is another mystery. Presumably he must have seen and been impressed by some of her Kalem productions, or perhaps Mae Marsh, who had appeared in two Kalem films for Kenean Buell in 1912, had become acquainted with Miriam and persuaded the director to let her join his company.

Miriam's first film for Griffith at Reliance-Majestic was in the Mae Marsh-Robert Harron sequence of *Home Sweet Home.* Miriam is the Easterner, who persuades Harron to leave Mae and return to the city with her. The issue of *Reel Life* quoted earlier said of Miss Cooper at Reliance-Majestic, "Two strong plays of hers are *When Fate Frowned* and *A Diamond in the Rough,* produced in the winter. Recently she won even greater distinction in *The Dishonored Medal, The Pseudo Prodigal* and in the great multiple reeler, *Home Sweet Home.*"

During this period, Griffith had been preparing to shoot *The Birth of a Nation,* and in *Photoplay* (October, 1916), Griffith explained why he had kept Miriam Cooper with his company. "Miss Cooper

I kept in the company for all the months between the idea that I might make the picture until the work began, because I knew she would be an exact 'Cameron' girl. Miriam Cooper was a perfect type of the beauty prevalent below the Mason and Dixon line." As the elder of the Cameron girls, Miss Cooper gives a good, solid performance. She is almost the stereotype elder sister, understanding and sympathetic yet firm.

While working on *The Birth of a Nation,* Miriam must have for the first time met Raoul Walsh, who portrayed John Wilkes Booth in the film. By the time *Intolerance* was completed, the two were engaged. They were married in Albuquerque, New Mexico, in 1916. The choice of this town was purely accidental; Miss Cooper was on her way to California from New York to wed Walsh, but he became so impatient that he set out to meet her. After an hour's stop in Albuquerque for the wedding, the couple resumed their journey westward.

Miriam Cooper's supreme acting achievement, without a doubt, was as "The Friendless One" in the modern story of *Intolerance.* Bessie Love recalled how Miriam began to bite her lip as she heard her lover seducing Mae Marsh in the locked room. So emotionally involved in her role was Miss Cooper that she drew blood. Bessie Love also recalled that the jump from the building after Miriam Cooper has shot the "Musketeer of the Slums" was doubled by an elderly Indian named "Eagle Eye" who used to hang around the Griffith set.

After completing *Intolerance,* Miriam planned to retire from the cinema and become a housewife, but Raoul Walsh had other ideas. "When we were married, I really planned to give up my work. However, just at that time Raoul began his first big production, *The Honor System,* and after trying to find the type he wanted for the girl, he grew discouraged and asked me to play it." From 1916 to 1919, Miriam appeared in only her husband's productions, films that included *The Silent Lie* (1917), *The Prussian Cur* (1918) and *Evangeline* (1919).

In his review of current pictures, Henry Dunn Cabot wrote in *Picture Play* (November, 1919): "Another picture which I admire for its sincerity is Longfellow's *Evangeline,* which has been given an excellent production by William Fox. The beautiful word pictures of the poem have been caught with remarkable appreciation by R. A. Walsh, who directed the play, and who saw to it that the characters of Evangeline, Gabriel, Basil—and all the others whom we have loved

Miriam Cooper in *Intolerance*. Julian Johnson wrote of her performance in *Photoplay:* "All actresses who honestly provide for home and baby by the business of vamping and gunning could do well to observe Miss Cooper's expressions and gestures. Miss Cooper is police dock—she is blotter transcript. Her face is what you *really* see some nights under the green lamps."

Intolerance: Robert Harron, Walter Long, and Miriam Cooper (frame enlargement)

Miriam Cooper in *Evangeline*

so well since we became acquainted with them in childhood—remain true to our own conception."

"The best results in any pictures are obtained when the director and the leading members of the cast work harmoniously together," said Miriam Cooper in 1920. "My husband knows me well enough to get the best work out of me, and I understand him so well that I know what effect he is striving for before he tells me. He is the best director I could possibly have, and of course I think he is the greatest director—he and Mr. Griffith." (18)

When Walsh left the Fox Company in 1920 for Realart, Miriam Cooper went with him to star in *The Deep Purple*. Then the couple transferred to First National, with *The Oath* (1921), *Serenade* (1921), and *Kindred of the Dust* (1922). "When my husband can't find anyone else to suit him, he puts me in his pictures—that's why I'm always in them," explained Miriam to *Motion Picture Magazine* (November, 1921).

But in 1924 she was divorced from Walsh, and in the same year she also made her last screen appearance, in Glenn Lyons's *Is Money Everything?* costarring opposite Norman Kerry. Miriam Cooper now lives in comparative luxury in Charlottesville, Virginia, in a farmhouse which she purchased nineteen years ago. She is currently at work on her autobiography, the publication of which is an eagerly awaited event.

Miriam Cooper was a totally Griffith-made star. Without a doubt she would be completely forgotten today had it not been for her roles in *The Birth of a Nation* and *Intolerance*. And Miss Cooper never forgot her debt to the director. She told Herbert Howe in 1922, "I *love* Mr. Griffith. Next to my husband, I love him more than any man in the world. He's so generous and sympathetic—so understanding— he knows everything—is always helping people." (31)

9

Clarine Seymour

An unfinished story.
—*Photoplay*

When writing of Clarine Seymour, I cannot help but recall an early
poem by Francis Thompson:

> The fairest things have fleetest end,
> Their scent survives their close.
> But the rose's scent is bitterness
> To him that loved the rose.

Beautiful, dark-haired Clarine, with the most bewitching pair of
eyes of any silent actress (*Picturegoer* described her as a "pocket
edition of Anita Stewart," but to me it seems unfair to compare her
unique talent and looks to any other actress) died at the age of
twenty-one at nine o'clock on the evening of Sunday, April 25, 1920.
She had just gained real stardom with her performance in *The Idol
Dancer*.

Born in Brooklyn of fairly wealthy parents, Clarine made her first
public appearance in an "entertainment" arranged by the New York
Avenue Methodist Church. In 1916 (this date was given by Clarine's
father in a letter to Edward Wagenknecht, but it should be pointed
out that all contemporary magazine articles give the date as 1917)

136

One of Clarine Seymour's earliest photographs

the family moved to New Rochelle, and in the same year, because of illness, Clarine's father was forced to liquidate his business. It was this misfortune that was to precipitate the girl's entry into films.

Clarine insisted that, in order to help out the family's finances,

Three Hours Late: Bobby Dunn and Clarine Seymour

she should go out to work, and promptly applied for, and obtained, a job with the Thanhouser Company, whose studios were in New Rochelle. Her playing in Thanhouser productions attracted the attention of the Pathe Company, who offered her a role in a Pearl White serial, and from this came a more important part in the Mollie King serial *The Mystery of the Double Cross*, released on March 18, 1917.

Pathe next issued an invitation to Clarine to work at their studios on the West Coast, an invitation which—despite a certain amount of family opposition—she accepted. The job, with Hal Roach's Rolin Comedy Company, called for her to appear in a series of films with Toto, the clown. The series was not a success, and Clarine was far from happy with Rolin. She refused to perform a certain stunt and a lawsuit followed, which Clarine eventually won, but it began to look as if her career was at an end before it had really begun.

However, she eventually obtained work with Al Christie, and became his leading lady in place of Billie Rhodes, who had joined her husband-to-be, "Smiling Billy" Parsons, in Capitol Comedies. Then, in the winter of 1918, she was introduced to D. W. Griffith. According to *Photoplay*, "Casting was beginning for *The Girl Who Stayed*

The upper part of
her sad — but the
feet still rag-time.

Clarine Seymour in *The Girl Who Stayed at Home* (frame enlargement)

True Heart Susie: Robert Harron, Clarine Seymour, and Lillian Gish

at Home. Two parts were wanted that would show the same opposite tendencies as the Gish sisters in *Hearts of the World*. Miss Gish was tired out, so Carol Dempster was given her chance to be a star. Dorothy was the logical type for the other part, but it so happened that Dorothy was being starred in her own Paramount productions.

And in walked Clarine, stretched to her full and glorious height of something just a trifle under five feet. A test was made and the help wanted sign was tucked away for the weeks to come."

The Girl Who Stayed at Home is generally dismissed as a minor Griffith production—largely because, one suspects, few critics or historians have ever bothered to view it. Admittedly, it opened on March 23, 1919 at New York's Strand Theater to a not too enthusiastic reception from the critics. *Wid's Film Daily* thought "To say *The Girl Who Stayed at Home* is disappointing might be going too far, because it contains many fine scenes, but in its entirety the picture does not equal a number of the producer's previous films, even those for which no special claims were made." However, about Clarine Seymour's Griffith debut the magazine had no reservations. "Miss Seymour is a real find, and her appearance in coming productions may be looked forward to with interest."

The main roles in the film were portrayed by Carol Dempster and Richard Barthelmess; Clarine Seymour and Robert Harron took the secondary roles of "Cutie Beautiful" and James Gray. "Cutie Beautiful" is a showgirl whose love and devotion make a man of the spineless Harron. (Harron's change to manhood is indicated by the loss of an extraordinary crab-like movement, which he sports throughout the first half of the film, and which presumably affected all spineless young Americans who preferred not to fight in the First World War.) Clarine's playing with Harron is a delight to watch; here at last, it seemed, was a team that could equal the Harron-Marsh partnership of earlier productions. But alas, the two were to appear together on the screen only one more time, and Harron was to die tragically only a matter of months before Clarine Seymour. The highlight of the film, for me at least, is the scene in which Clarine is desperately trying to concentrate her thoughts on her knitting and the horrors of war that Harron must be facing, while the gramophone at her side, playing a jazz record, steals the attention of her feet. A title summed it up well, as only a Griffith title could: "The upper part of her sad—but the feet still rag-time."

Immediately after completing *The Girl Who Stayed at Home,* Clarine began work on *True Heart Susie,* again playing a secondary role, but this time that of "the other woman." It would be wrong to give undue prominence to Miss Seymour's role, for the film belongs undoubtedly to Lillian Gish—it is one of her finest performances. Suffice it to say that it would be impossible to imagine anyone else in the role of "The Little Milliner from Chicago" except Clarine Seymour. She is splendid as she leads Harron into matrimony, and no one could blame him for believing. "Those great eyes can hold only truth."

True Heart Susie is a sentimental story of rural America, with Lillian Gish as the local girl who secretly loves neighbour Robert Harron, and pays—at a sacrifice to herself—for him to go to college and train as a clergyman. On his return to the village, Harron is ensnared by Clarine Seymour, and only after Seymour's death (caused by her unfaithfulness to him in attending a friend's party secretly and so being drenched in a sudden storm on her return) does Harron realise which girl has loved him since childhood. Even at the end, Harron is not aware of Clarine's unfaithfulness: "She died as she had lived—a little unfaithful." I said earlier that *True Heart Susie* is Lillian Gish's film, but it also belongs to Robert Harron; for his performance in this, his penultimate film for Griffith, proves his capabilities as an actor as he grows from adolescent boy to mature man,

Scarlet Days: Clarine Seymour protects her lover (Richard Barthelmess) from the sheriff in the only way she knows

and give the lie to some critics who have labeled him a "ham" actor.

In Europe the film is recognised as the masterwork it is, but in the United States it is little thought of and little seen. Its precursors are the Griffith Biograph productions such as *A Country Cupid* (released July 24, 1911), in which Blanche Sweet played the schoolmistress, loved and subsequently threatened by the village idiot. Writing in *Harper's Bazaar* in 1940, Lillian Gish commented that the story "was borrowed from Charles Dickens, and was, in fact, the Agnes and Dora story from *David Copperfield*. I was playing Agnes. It was my last film with Robert Harron, the David of the film. Clarine Seymour, who at seventeen seemed destined to become one of the most beloved stars, if her exposure to the cold in the winter scenes of *Way Down East* had not hastened her untimely death, was Dora." (23) (There is no documentary proof as to Miss Gish's assertion regarding Clarine's death.)

Following *True Heart Susie,* Clarine embarked on another picture, in which she costarred with Carol Dempster—*Scarlet Days*. The film is a Western, set at the time of the 1849 California Gold Rush; it is mercifully a fairly short film. I say mercifully, for it must qualify as one of the worst features Griffith ever directed. In an orgy of melodramatic acting, Clarine Seymour's performance is a blessed relief—even when she is indulging in such unlikely escapades as butting a goat, a would-be suitor, or the local sheriff.

The interior scenes look as if they would be more in keeping with an Edison one-reeler, and the film's only redeeming feature (aside from Miss Seymour) would appear to be its picturesque locations. Griffith seems to have borrowed heavily from earlier works; the besieged cabin, for example, was used in *The Battle at Elderbush Gulch* and *The Birth of a Nation* (where it was done better). When Carol Dempster and Eugenie Besserer (playing her mother) hide under the floorboards just as the Cameron women did in *The Birth of a Nation,* Miss Dempster giggles hysterically exactly as Mae Marsh had done five years earlier.

Criticism of the film was mixed. *Wid's Film Daily* commented: "There is no question about it. David Wark Griffith is an artist. He has taken a simple, crude, little Western melodrama and made it a picture so true to life, so realistic, that for the time it is running on the screen one is lifted completely out of this life and transported back to the days of '49." *Variety,* on the other hand, thought that "*Scarlet Days* as a story was not worthy of Griffith's direction in picturization. . . . It is entirely commonplace." But all critics were

The Idol Dancer: Creighton Hale, Clarine Seymour, and Richard Barthelmess

The Idol Dancer: Clarine Seymour, Kate Bruce, George McQuarrie, and Creighton Hale

united in their praise of Clarine Seymour. *Photoplay* wrote, "The picturesque little Seymour, in her adorable description of Chiquita, the hot-tamale vampire of intense ardor and no soap, runs away with most of the laughter and enthusiasm." *Variety* decided that "she appears to have all the exquisite piquancy that made the public love Dorothy Gish. She is the outstanding girl of the present picture." And *The Morning Telegraph* summed it all up with its comment, "Clarine Seymour is splendid."

Late in 1919, Clarine began work on her first film as a star, *The Idol Dancer;* it was also to be her last. *The Idol Dancer* is set—as the opening title romantically tells us—"On Rainbow Beach, a Romance Island under the Southern Cross." Clarine plays "White Almond Flower" ("Blood of vivacious France, inscrutable Java and languorous Samoa mingle in her veins"), but to her guardian, Old Thomas, and to the white people on the island she is plain (if any character that Clarine played can be described as plain) Mary. She is "a curious little creature of boldness, yet timidity," who has attracted two men on the island—a beachcomber admirably played by Richard Barthelmess, "a derelict thrown upon the shore by shifting waves and winds of many adventures," and Walter Kincaid (played by Creighton Hale, about whose acting probably the least said the better), "an invalid, whose greatest moral offense has been kissing his cousin in a dark hallway, for which he has been duly repentant." Clarine's dancing attracts both men to her; it also attracts a tribe of cannibals who attack the island while Barthelmess is away fishing. The girl is saved from the horde by Creighton Hale, who gives up his life for her, thus leaving the way clear for Richard Barthelmess, who arrives in the nick of time to claim Clarine as his bride. So, as the final title tells us in language that could only have been written by a D. W. Griffith, "They tread at last the warm white path of velvet moonflowers to the land of Dreams Fulfilled."

The Idol Dancer cannot be described as one of the director's major works; it can hardly be described as one of his better minor works. Griffith went on location to the South Seas to shoot the picture, but he might just as well have stayed at his Mamaroneck studios. The film is a waste of the talents of a group of fine players and a fine director.

It was Clarine Seymour's performance that the critics noticed. *Exhibitors' Herald* found her "more fascinating than ever," *The Dramatic Mirror* thought that "the redeeming features of the film are the very picturesque views of the sea interwoven wherever possible and the vivacity of Clarine Seymour's acting." Burns Mantle in

Clarine Seymour: The Last Portrait (courtesy of Edward Wagenknecht)

Photoplay said of her: "She wears not so very much in front and a little less than 'alf of that be'ind, as the gifted Rudyard phrased it, and she is a beauty bright from the bells on her toes to the permanent wave in her hair (a wave she never learned to do in the South Seas Islands). Moreover she not only negotiates the hula with considerable grace, but she plays the dramatic scenes with enough fire and sincerity almost to convince you that she is what she pretends to be, a dusky island belle."

Poor little Clarine did not enjoy her popularity long. As the film was released, she died. Many of the reviews, including the one from *Photoplay,* appeared a month or more after her passing. Within a matter of hours after a new four-year contract (which would have assured her of an income during that period of two million dollars), was drawn up, the fame she had secured mattered nothing to her. She was not seen again—although she had in fact begun work on *Way Down East,* playing the role subsequently taken over by Mary Hay, and according to Edward Wagenknecht may still be glimpsed in some of the long shots in the film.*

In its July, 1920 issue, *Photoplay* published an article by Betty Shannon, who wrote, "There was a very different sort of story written to fill this space. It was the story of a vivid, very much alive young person to whom success had come after several years of particular discouragement and difficulty. It was the story of a warm, unspoiled, friendly girl. But the story of Clarine Seymour had to be stopped short and taken from the presses." (50) The piece was headed "An Unfinished Story." I can think of no more fitting epitaph for an actress who I feel sure would have become as important a star to D. W. Griffith as Lillian Gish, and who might very well have made the director's final films as great as his earlier works.

---

* Edward Wagenknecht points out to me that he took Lillian Gish's word for this. He could not say he has ever recognized her himself.

10

Carol Dempster

He'd given up his throne for a third-rate actress.
—Adela Rogers St. Johns

The Carol Dempster controversy has raged on and off for almost
fifty years. Was Griffith's insistence on starring her in his films the
reason for his downfall, or was he already slipping and failing in his
creative abilities? As far as Griffith's other leading ladies are concerned, Carol Dempster was exclusively to blame. If they talk of her
at all, they describe her with contradictory words such as "ambitious"
and "stupid." When I bluntly asked Anita Loos if Carol Dempster
was responsible for Griffith's downfall, she replied, "Well, she certainly didn't do him any good."

Miss Dempster was far from popular, either, with non-Griffith
actresses. One well-known Paramount star of the twenties commented
to me: "I never cared for her. She had sharp features, you know, and
I always used to say she was as sharp off screen as she was on. She
was working at the Paramount, Long Island, Studios, and I was working there with Bebe [Daniels], and Bebe would say, 'Do you get on
with that Carol?' And I'd say, 'No.' And she'd say, 'Same here!'"
As far as Carol Dempster was concerned, it mattered little what her
fellow actresses thought of her then, and today it matters little what

Carol Dempster

history makes of her or her films. She lives in quiet retirement in La Jolla, California, and does not mix with any of the film set.

Personalities aside, however, posterity will judge the Dempster films on her performances. What can one say of those performances? She gives very good impersonations of Mae Marsh, Lillian Gish, and even Dorothy Gish (in *Dream Street*), but that is all her performances generally are—impersonations. In only one film, *The Sorrows of Satan,* does she give an original and, subsequently, a fine performance. One good acting role in eleven pictures is not a very fine record.

Carol Dempster was born in Duluth, Minnesota, on either December 9, 1901 or January 6, 1902, the youngest of four children of a Great Lakes captain and his wife. For reasons unknown, her father tired of his occupation and moved with his family to California. While dancing at a school "entertainment," Miss Dempster was spotted by Ruth St. Denis. As Carol recalled for W. Adolphe Roberts in *Motion Picture Magazine* (July, 1925): "I began as a dancer, you know—out in California with Ruth St. Denis. I was the youngest pupil to graduate in her first class. We were to go on tour, and I

Carol Dempster in *The Girl Who Stayed at Home* (frame enlargement)

actually started and appeared for two weeks in San Francisco. I was forced to drop out because of illness in the family. When I went south again, it was to find that Mr. Griffith had noticed me among Miss St. Denis's girls. He asked me if I'd like to go into motion pictures. Since it was a chance to work with him, I went, of course."

In actual fact, prior to the tour, Miss Dempster had already worked for D. W. Griffith, as one of the dancers in the Babylonian sequence of *Intolerance.* Her first real role in a Griffith production was as the New York girl who wants to go dancing with Robert Harron in *A Romance of Happy Valley.* This she followed with a supporting role to Dorothy Gish in *The Hope Chest,* directed by Elmer Clifton. Both films were released by Paramount-Artcraft in 1919. Unfortunately, history does not record whether Griffith suggested Dempster to Dorothy Gish for the role in *The Hope Chest,* or whether the choice was entirely Dorothy's.

Carol was to play one more minor role in *True Heart Susie* before her first featured part in *The Girl Who Stayed at Home.* In *True Heart Susie,* Carol is one of Clarine Seymour's fun-loving friends, the one who is ultimately responsible for Robert Harron knowing exactly how Clarine contracted pneumonia. In each of these early films, Carol Dempster's playing was more than adequate for the roles she was taking, although it is hard to say, on the basis of them alone, whether she had the ability to sustain a longer and more demanding performance.

As I have said in the chapter on Clarine Seymour, the role of Acoline France in *The Girl Who Stayed at Home* was originally to have been played by Lillian Gish, but, as she was over-tired, it went to Carol Dempster. Undoubtedly, Carol was unsuited to the part of the virginal heroine threatened with rape by a German soldier (shades of *Hearts of the World*), and so, perhaps, it is a little unfair to judge her too harshly. Certainly at the time critics were not unimpressed by her performance. *Photoplay* (August, 1919) wrote of her, "The prime reason Miss Dempster has become identified with the list of Griffith players is because she is: First, probably the most graceful in movement of any young woman now in pictures. Second, she has a peculiar type of beauty that appeals to many people. Third, she has a case of real inside sincerity that the camera does not fail to register."

It is difficult to argue with *Photoplay* on any of these counts. She was graceful: after all, she had trained as a dancer, and had a dancer's natural grace of movement. She did appeal to the public, and in an unusual way: Delight Evans, writing in *Photoplay* in 1922, posed the question, "You may think you don't like her in pictures. But you

The Love Flower: Carol Dempster and Richard Barthelmess

will go to see her again. How do you explain that?" Only on the
third count can one honestly disagree with *Photoplay*. If she did have
inside sincerity, it was so far inside that it was completely invisible to
the film viewer.

After *The Girl Who Stayed at Home* came *Scarlet Days*, about

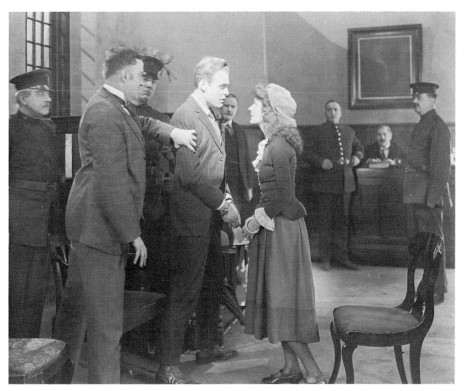

Dream Street: Ralph Graves and Carol Dempster

Carol Dempster is menaced in *One Exciting Night*.

which it is perhaps best to leave one's thoughts unspoken. Its only interest lies in the fact that here for the first time Carol Dempster seemed openly to imitate other Griffith players, in this case Mae Marsh and Lillian Gish. Indeed, *The Morning Telegraph* of November 16, 1919, noted, "Carol Dempster, under Mr. Griffith's direction, is a sort of composite of Lillian Gish and Mae Marsh since she employs a number of Miss Gish's nervous little mannerisms and has one scene which recalls Miss Marsh's big moment in *The Birth of a Nation*."

The Love Flower, which opened at New York's Strand Theater on August 22, 1920, was Carol's first solo starring production. The film's theme is that peace and tolerance are only possible away from civilization, and that love will "forgive these deeds done for its sake." Miss Dempster and her father live on an idyllic South Sea island whose peace is shattered when Dempster's lover, Richard Barthelmess, unwittingly brings her father's pursuer to the island. The film contains some ridiculous scenes, as for example, when Dempster tells her father that "I saw a man," he nervously inquires, "Did he look like an officer?" and she simply giggles and hugs him. There are endless posings for close-ups, particularly on the River of Hyacinths, and Miss Dempster at times runs all over the place in the most hysterical fashion. One can hardly blame her father for remarking, "Do stop running around here like an idiot." In all fairness, however, it must be pointed out that Miss Dempster's acting is as nothing compared to the melodramatics of Florence Short, who, at the death of her lover, tears at her hair and generally behaves like a lunatic.

The film does contain some beautiful underwater sequences in which Carol, "straining and swaying in youth's hot madness," shows to some advantage her body and her swimming abilities. Later in the film these same underwater sequences are repeated, but now "she uses her skill for a deadly purpose," as she tries to drown the detective come to arrest her father.

Burns Mantle, writing in *Photoplay* (November, 1920), gives his opinion of Miss Dempster, an opinion that must have been shared by many other critics at this time. "If Mr. Griffith wishes us to become well-acquainted with his latest discovery he will not be disappointed. We have seen Carol Dempster through the misty close-up and under water; we have seen her outlined against the sky, the wind whipping her filmy costume about her. We have seen her one expression for love, hate, fear, and the other cardinal emotions. As an actress Miss Dempster is an excellent high diver." However, in recent years two

Carol Dempster in *America*

critics have praised the film and Miss Dempster's performance. John Dorr, writing in *Cinema* (Fall, 1971), discusses the film in detail, trying to prove that the Dempster-Griffith relationship was more important than the Gish-Griffith combination; he fails in that his basic premise, that Dempster "had a formidable acting talent," has no

Carol Dempster in *The White Rose*

foundation. William K. Everson has described *The Love Flower* as "a good Carol Dempster vehicle." (21)

For a year, Carol Dempster was not prominent on the cinema screens of the world, although she might be just glimpsed in *Way Down East*. But in 1921, she returned in another Griffith-Dempster disaster, *Dream Street.* As both films were based on writings of Thomas Burke, it seems natural to compare *Dream Street* to *Broken Blossoms,* but of course they have little or nothing in common. Lillian Gish, the frightened, tormented waif of the latter, bears little resemblance to the hard, steel-nerved Miss Dempster, who shows no fear of Ralph Graves's advances and who tells the threatening Chinaman, "After this you let white girls alone." The film's most ludicrous moment is surely the scene of the fire in the theater, when Carol quells a panic with some dancing which seems more panic-stricken than the theater audience.

Dream Street also introduces a new Carol Dempster impersonation, one of Dorothy Gish—and a very passable impersonation it is. It is most apparent in the comic scene of Carol trying to mount a mule, one of the film's brighter moments. *Dream Street* is undoubtedly overlong and contains far too many close-ups of Griffith's protégée, but it is not perhaps a total disaster, and deserves a revival. The close-ups were what the critics noticed. *Photoplay* (July, 1921) commented, "D. W. slips into the habit of holding his close-ups so long the character itself fades and you hear nothing but the stentorian tones of the director himself shouting: 'Hold it, Carol!' 'Get the terror into it, Ralph!' 'For God's sake, weep a little, Charlie!' Or if you know nothing of the methods of picture-taking, you wonder just why you must be shown again and again how the heroine looks when she is in trouble and mightily upset about it."

After *Dream Street,* Carol Dempster made her only non-Griffith twenties picture *Sherlock Holmes* (British title: *Moriarty*). Miss Dempster told Gladys Hall of *Motion Picture Magazine* (July, 1922): "I wouldn't do just *any* picture. I didn't even care, at first, to play in *Sherlock Holmes* with John Barrymore. But Mr. Griffith approved it, and all of my friends argued in favor of it, and now I am glad that I did it. Curiously enough, I had never seen Mr. Barrymore either on the stage or the screen. I told him that when he telephoned me about the picture and he said, 'Perhaps you have *heard* of me!' I thought he might not want me after that—but he did. He had seen me, it seems, in *Dream Street* and thought that we were much the same physical type. Built long, I suppose he meant!"

Carol Dempster was introduced as a love interest in the film, which was released on October 29, 1922. Robert E. Sherwood wrote of its director, "Albert Parker reproduced the thrill of the original stories both in his action and his characterization." The English magazine, *Kine Weekly,* commented, "Carol Dempster is charming in the small part of Alice."

After completing *Sherlock Holmes*, Carol returned to Griffith for what many consider—perhaps rightly—was his poorest work, *One Exciting Night*. Griffith was obviously aware of its weaknesses, as he was overly eager to praise the film, while at the same time asking audiences to excuse it. He was quoted in the *New York Tribune* (November 12, 1922): "Perhaps this picture appears like a hastily made work. It is the exact opposite. There is no more difficult thing than to put suspense and mystery on the screen. . . . Personally I think such scenes as the storm scene are the special province of the films, the first medium that has been able to reproduce this elemental drama that is so tremendous. The awe of storms is in us from ten thousand years of memories. A storm is a magnificent beauty; it is a great drama. How can you compare some pitiful sex problem with the scene of a tree that has stood for a hundred years sturdy against all attacks suddenly being uprooted and tossed away to a dying death? We, of course, like to think that our own little affairs are important, but there certainly is something affecting in the destruction of a great healthy tree that was in its prime before we were born. . . . I like *One Exciting Night*. I like its comedy. I like several things about it. I like it because I feel that it will take many people out of themselves during the minutes they are seeing it. And anything that does that is worth liking." The storm sequence, in which a tree takes what seems to be an eternity to fall upon Carol Dempster, was filmed during an actual storm in the Westchester Hills on the night of June 11, 1922.

One Exciting Night contains what is probably the most ludicrous scene in any D. W. Griffith production, where Carol Dempster is shown tied to an altar, following the title, "Youth sacrificed on the altars of greed and passion." Criticism of the film was very mixed, although no critic went so far as to condemn it. *Motion Picture News* (October 21, 1922) thought, "Carol Dempster, who, always good, is in this production, showing the hand of the 'Wizard' himself. She should take her place among the highest after *One Exciting Night*." Al Jolson told the *New York American* (November 21, 1922), "It is poetry. If the picture were twenty reels long, I couldn't get enough of it, particularly the comedy of Mr. Porter Strong." However, Laurence Reid in *Motion Picture Classic* contended, "We expect bigger things from the man who gave us *Broken Blossoms, Way Down East, Intolerance,* and *The Birth of a Nation*." And Robert E. Sherwood in the *New York Herald* (October 24, 1922) wrote, "*One Exciting Night* is in reality a pot boiler—and a highly successful one at that. It will do well in the box office where it goes. Mr. Griffith often has to devote his attention to pictures like this, because it is an open secret that some of his more ambitious offerings have not been quite as profitable as they might be. . . . Let us trust, then, that *One Exciting Night* will make enough money to pay for another *Broken Blossoms*."

Sadly, *One Exciting Night* did not make enough money to finance another *Broken Blossoms*. The film was not a great box office success, and it was not a *Broken Blossoms* that followed, but *The White Rose*. Thanks to the fine playing of Mae Marsh, *The White Rose* does stand out as a minor Griffith masterpiece, but it and Griffith's next film, *America,* gave no indication that Carol Dempster was developing any talents as an actress.

Then came *Isn't Life Wonderful*. Shot mainly in Germany at the little town of Kopenick, on the outskirts of Berlin, *Isn't Life Wonderful* was based on a story by a British Army major, Geoffrey Moss. At the time he was quoted as saying about his collection of short stories, collected together in book form as *Defeat*—"My book was merely a cry for fair play. The story is the sincerest thing I have ever done. I tried to impart a beauty that is all around us, wherever we are. It was a beauty which I could feel always, but could see but dimly."

"A beauty which I could feel always, but could see but dimly." How many critics must have echoed those words when they saw Carol Dempster's performance in that film for the first time. "At first we could hardly believe our eyes," commented *Photoplay*. "Inga was our own Carol Dempster. But as Inga crawls over to Hans and whispers, 'I have you and you have me and, oh—isn't life wonderful?' we felt like standing up and shouting, 'It is!'" "Miss Dempster gives one of the finest performances ever seen on the screen," wrote *Moving Picture World*. And the *New York World* (December 1, 1924) agreed, "Its leading woman gives one of the finest performances I have seen in pictures. It may be the very best."

The innermost theme of *Isn't Life Wonderful* is love. As the opening title states, "This simple story shows that love makes beautiful all it touches." It is the tale of a family of Polish refugees, who are described as "war's harvest," just as the dead on the battlefields of *The Birth of a Nation* represented "war's peace." We first see Carol Dempster with her grandmother; she is very plain and subdued, with her hair pulled tightly back. Dempster has so many fine scenes in the film, that it is difficult to single out one or two. But she is particularly appealing in two episodes with her grandmother: in one where she is trying to persuade the old lady to eat turnips, and in

Isn't Life Wonderful: Carol Dempster waits hopefully in the line at the butcher's shop as the price of meat slowly rises

another where Neil Hamilton announces that he and Dempster want to get married, and there is a cut to a close-up of Carol's face as the grandmother demands, "And what about the babies?" In a particularly harrowing scene, Dempster, in line for meat outside the butcher's shop, watches the price of a cut of beef gradually rise until it is beyond her financial means.

So overwhelming is the emotion in much of the film that one feels genuine pleasure when the refugees sit down to a "real" supper of potatoes, liverwurst, and (for the grandmother) one poached egg. The final scenes between Hamilton and Dempster also contain an overpowering emotional content, as Hamilton in despair, with the couple's only valuable possession—a cartload of potatoes—stolen, turns to Carol and mutters, "Nothing is of any use." It is perhaps unfortunate that Griffith chose to tag on to the film a happy scene of the newlyweds moving into their own cottage, since the viewer feels sufficient contentment in Dempster's cry that their having each other makes life wonderful.

Isn't Life Wonderful was not a financial success. It was drab, and drab films were just what the public did not want in the fun-loving twenties. Typical of the reaction of the "popular" critics was Iris N. Carpenter's writing in the English *Picture Show*: "Pictures, whatever we may say concerning their art and theme, are designed first and foremost for the provision of entertainment—or they should be. There is enough poverty and misery in life itself, without paying for the privilege of seeing it depicted on the screen." Griffith was forced to sign a contract with Famous Players-Lasky, and his disinterest is only too apparent in his next two productions, *Sally of the Sawdust* and *That Royle Girl,* for both of which films Miss Dempster provided mediocre performances. It seemed as if the genuine talent she had displayed for emotional acting in *Isn't Life Wonderful* was just a flash in the pan. And then came what was to be her final screen appearance in *The Sorrows of Satan*.

I believe that critics in years to come will dismiss *Isn't Life Won-*

Isn't Life Wonderful: The gang of ruffians seize the cartload of potatoes from Neil Hamilton and Carol Dempster

derful, and accept *The Sorrows of Satan* as the definitive Carol Dempster performance. Based on the once-popular novel by Marie Corelli, *The Sorrows of Satan* concerns one Geoffrey Tempest (Ricardo Cortez), who loves Mavis Clare (Carol Dempster) but who, desiring riches for the both of them, sells his soul to the Devil (Adolphe Menjou). In the end Tempest returns to Mavis, whose faith in God drives away the Devil. The story is trite, old-fashioned and melodramatic; many would have supposed that in the hands of D. W. Griffith it would appear even more melodramatic and old-fashioned. But on the contrary, Griffith turned out a brilliant, sophisticated production, and Carol Dempster gave the performance of her career.

Here at last is Carol Dempster, the actress, as she sits across from Ricardo Cortez, listening to the poem he has written, inspired by her beauty: "I couldn't have inspired that, it's too beautiful"; here is the girl who believes in the morning that the night of love with Cortez is not the beginning of romance, but the end; here is the hysterical child who chases after Cortez as he drives away in Menjou's car, and stands still for one long, wistful close-up when she realises that she has lost him.

Isn't Life Wonderful received good reviews, but was bad box office; *The Sorrows of Satan* was the reverse. *Photoplay,* while considering Carol Dempster "excellent," thought the production "old-fashioned." *Motion Picture Classic* was "frankly disappointed," and suggested "that Mr. Griffith be given simpler stories about people who do not revel in Bacchanalian orgies." However, the magazine continued, "It is for Carol Dempster that we save our best adjectives. And for Griffith too. He has made of Miss Dempster a splendid actress . . . an artist." One or two writers were delighted that at last critics were beginning to recognize that Carol Dempster was not without talent. Dorothy Herzog, writing in *Photoplay,* declared "Carol Dempster has suffered for years from the refined torture of comparison and prejudice."

However, success came too late for Carol. No more films were considered suitable to her talents, and (to be more directly honest) the companies now employing Griffith had no time for Miss Dempster. Carol was unperturbed. "I don't care to work for anybody but Mr. Griffith. When he has a part which he thinks is my type I suppose I will play it. I wouldn't worry if I never played in another picture."

On August 15, 1929, Carol married a New York banker, Edwin S. Larsen. It was obvious that she would never return to films. Some years ago, she told Richard Lamparski, "I just never think about my

The Sorrows of Satan: Adolphe Menjou and Carol Dempster

days in pictures. I am always surprised that anyone remembers me. It was so long ago. So many of my movies were so sad. Maybe my fans would like to know that in real life Carol Dempster had a happy ending."

11

The Last of the Griffith Line

The end of any great man's career is always a sad event—particularly when it is tinged with bitterness and frustration. To such an end came the film career of D. W. Griffith. After completing *The Sorrows of Satan,* he directed only five more features, *Drums of Love* and *The Battle of the Sexes* (both in 1928), *Lady of the Pavements* (1929), *Abraham Lincoln* (1930) and *The Struggle* (1931). Two of those films, *Lady of the Pavements* and *The Struggle,* we can see today not only as the fine films that they are, but also as productions which carried on the tradition of the Griffith heroine.

Of course, there were other actresses in the twenties—actresses now forgotten—who might have been Griffith girls. In his stock company at the Mamaroneck Studios were two actresses whom Griffith obviously had in mind to groom as future leading ladies: Betty Jewel and Riza Royce. Betty Jewel did in fact achieve stardom as a leading lady in Westerns, playing opposite Gary Cooper in *The Last Outlaw* and *Arizona Bound* and opposite Jack Holt in *The Mysterious Rider,* all released in 1927. She appeared very briefly in *Orphans of the Storm,* and apparently was always so much in evidence on location that she was nicknamed "Griffith's Third Orphan." Riza Royce is now probably best remembered, if she is remembered at all, as the

164

Lupe Velez

Lupe Velez (*The Lady of the Pavements*) is presented to her patroness, Jetta Goudal

one-time wife of Josef von Sternberg. Miss Royce's statement to *Motion Picture Magazine* (November, 1925) is typical of many actresses' loyalty to Griffith. "All that I am, or expect to be, turns upon my experience under Griffith. When the stock company was disbanded, I simply wouldn't look for another job for a long, long time. I couldn't bear to think of working for anyone but Mr. Griffith."

For his leading lady in *Lady of the Pavements,* which opened at the United Artists Theater, Los Angeles, on January 22, 1929 and the Rialto Theater, New York, on March 9, 1929, Griffith chose the tempestuous star, Lupe Velez. Born Guadalupe Villalobos Velez on July 18, 1910 in the small Mexican town of San Luis Potosi, Lupe Velez began her career at the age of fifteen as a dancer in a musical show in Mexico City. She achieved film stardom as a result of her performance opposite Douglas Fairbanks, Sr. in *The Gaucho.* Her popularity continued until her death on December 14, 1944 from an overdose of sleeping pills.

Velez demonstrates all the attributes of a Griffith heroine, but in her own inimitable style. And it was Lupe Velez and her acting that the critics noticed. *Variety* commented, "Lupe Velez gets everything in the picture; nine-tenths of the close-ups are hers although she is third in the billing." John S. Cohen, Jr. in *The New York Sun* remarked, "One is reminded of the gosling days of the Gishes and the Dempsters." Lupe is a prostitute chosen by Jetta Goudal, out of spite for William Boyd, to be groomed as a lady with whom Boyd will fall in love and marry, only to discover after the wedding her real identity—the plot, as Eileen Bowser has pointed out, has its origins in a story by Diderot. Our first glimpse of Lupe Velez is typically Griffith—in a halo formed by an artist's cloak. The scene in which Franklin Pangborn tries to teach her to be a lady contains typical elements of Griffith comedy, but they are given a new sparkle by the radiant Miss Velez.

Lady of the Pavements was released as a part-talkie; the talking sequences, in fact, consisted of Lupe Velez singing "Where Is the Song of Songs for Me?" composed by Irving Berlin, "At the Dance," and "Nena." It is an interesting footnote that Hollywood, the town which treated Griffith so shabbily during his lifetime, has changed not at all. *Lady of the Pavements* was screened at Grauman's Chinese Theater on Thursday, November 11, 1971, at a public performance attended by, among others, Jetta Goudal. The typically Hollywood audience spent most of the film's 85 minutes jeering and hooting with derision.

Much has been written—most of it derogatory—about Griffith's final cinematic bow, *The Struggle*. And that is unfortunate, for the film contains many things that are praiseworthy, not least of which is the acting of Zita Johann. Born in Hungary on July 14, 1904, Miss Johann came to New York at the age of seven. After attending Bryant High School, she joined the Alvienne School of the Theater, and then the Theater Guild; she made her first public appearance in the Guild's production of *Man and the Masses* at New York's Garrick Theater on April 14, 1924. She had two major stage successes, playing with Clark Gable in *Machinal* and in Philip Barry's *Tomorrow and Tomorrow*. Then, as she recalled for Dena Reed, "John Emerson came round to my dressing room one evening last season and asked how I'd like to go into the movies. I said I wouldn't. Then he told me Mr. Griffith was going to direct and related something of the story. It was the sort of thing I liked—and who wouldn't like the idea of being launched under Griffith?" (41)

Griffith financed the film himself, for distribution through United

Artists. Anita Loos, who with her husband John Emerson wrote the script, recalled for me: "I think all of it was Griffith's idea. Anything that Griffith did at that point would only be considered as a Griffith film. I knew it was a soap opera, and I knew it was no good, but I just put down what he wanted me to, and it was actually his story. I think everything about the picture was his own. I think all the time he was shooting it I was away. And I felt terribly sad about him, because I had a premonition that it was going to be a terrible flop, and it worried me. And I think it worried me to the extent that I just kept away."

The Struggle opened at New York's Rivoli Theater on Tuesday, December 10, 1931. The advertisements for the film particularly mentioned the leading man, Hal Skelly. "Skelly! Mark that name well! This one picture will send him zooming to motion picture stardom just as Griffith's previous triumphs sent blazing to the cinema heavens such names as Gish! Pickford! Valentino! Barthelmess!" The

The Struggle: D. W. Griffith explains a scene to Zita Johann

film was a disaster. *The Daily News* reported, "Last night's premiere audience tittered audibly." "Last night was Old Biograph week at the Rivoli," commented the *New York Evening Post,* "with David Wark Griffith disporting himself in a nostalgic orgy of the choicest moments from his flicker creations, including everything from *The Birth of a Nation* to the nickelodeon thrillers." Julia Shawell in the *Evening Graphic* wrote, "I weep for Mr. Griffith and this blight on his brilliant film record." While *Photoplay* commented simply, "Directed by D. W. Griffith, who sixteen years ago made *The Birth of a Nation.*"

Viewing *The Struggle* today, it is impossible to accept that the film deserved such criticism. Its theme of what alcoholism can do to a person is as modern today as it was—or should have been—in 1931. *The Struggle* opens with a prologue set in 1911, a delightfully nostalgic prologue; one character asks "Have you seen the Biograph Girl. I wonder what her name is?" And Griffith in this prologue introduces something new to sound films, something which we now accept as perfectly natural in films, overlapping dialogue—even in 1931 Griffith was still the innovator. The film then advances to 1923, with America at the height of prohibition. Zita Johann is the typically sweet, innocent Griffith heroine who marries a man to whom drink seems the only escape from his problems. And here again Griffith is the innovator. He takes the camera out of the studio (the film was, in fact, photographed at the "new" Biograph Studios on 175th Street) and into the streets of the Bronx. It really seems extraordinary that one newspaper, *The Daily News,* should criticize the film because "the sets are cheap and the street scenes are recognizably Bronx ones." Of course the sets are cheap; this is a story of a working class family. And of course the street scenes are recognizably Bronx ones; the story is set in the Bronx. One suspects that too many of the critics of this era were used to the style of living depicted in the films of Norma Shearer and Corinne Griffith.

Some critics today have carped at much of the dialogue, and used as a particular example the final line uttered by Zita Johann, "Jimmie, your eyes are all shiny." Yet what is wrong with this line? What else could there be for a wife to say, gazing with love at her husband, who at last really belongs just to her.

Zita Johann came in for much mixed criticism. Richard Murray in the *Standard Union* thought, "Miss Johann screens well and her voice registers affectively. With the proper material, she should acquire a large fan mail." While Richard Watts, Jr., writing in the *New York Herald Tribune,* commented, "Miss Zita Johann is utterly lost in the incredible action and dialogue." Miss Johann herself remarked: "Working with Mr. Griffith has been wonderful. Like Mr. Hopkins [Arthur Hopkins had produced *Machinal* on the stage], he lets me interpret my own way, but he is extremely sensitive and if I do something that does not satisfy me, he knows immediately and orders a retake. You know there are two kinds of acting—interpretive, where you follow the director's interpretation, and creative, where you create the character as you think it should be done. I can only do creative acting—anything else hampers me." (41)

After completing *The Struggle,* Miss Johann was put under contract to MGM, but did not make a picture for that company. She did, however, appear in a number of productions elsewhere: Howard Hawks's *Tiger Shark* (1932), Karl Freund's *The Mummy* (1932), Lothar Mendes's *Luxury Liner* (1933), and Irving Cummings's *Grand Canary* (1934). Zita Johann was far happier, and certainly far more successful, on the stage, and she soon departed from films.

D. W. Griffith never again directed an entire feature. He is said to have worked on *San Francisco,* although Anita Loos told me that she was present on the set during most of the shooting, and she was never aware of his being present at any time. In late 1939, Griffith was signed by Hal Roach to direct *One Million B.C.,* but Griffith later left the production. He explained, "Mr. Roach did not feel that it was necessary to give the characters as much individuality as I thought was needed, and so I did not wish to appear responsible for the picture by having my name on it. My name would do the film little good, and I am sure that the picture would do me little good."

David Wark Griffith died in Hollywood on July 23, 1948. At that time several of his actresses spoke of just what he had meant to them and to their careers. Mae Marsh told the *Los Angeles Examiner,* "It is as though my father had gone. Our beloved D. W. not only taught us everything we knew, he guided our hearts. The world knows how he influenced our careers. But only we can know how he molded our spirit." Norma Talmadge also spoke to the same newspaper: "My sister, Constance, and I are grateful that we were once part of the family of actors who learned everything from the greatest leader the screen has ever known."

And at the memorial service at Hollywood's Masonic Temple on July 27, 1948, Donald Crisp, representing all those who had worked with and under David Wark Griffith, summed it up. "D. W. created a whole generation of stars. All of us know their names, and they became the backbone of a growing industry. Pictures thrived and

D. W. Griffith visits his greatest star, Lillian Gish, on the set of *Duel in the Sun*

grew on the strength of personalities he had discovered. For while the world has lost a sad and lonely legendary figure, we have lost a friend."

Appendix 1
The British Names of American Biograph Players

Because of American Biograph's policy of not releasing the names of their players, and because of the British filmgoing public's demand to know the names, M.P. Sales, British distributors of American Biograph productions, invented names for the Biograph company. The following is the first complete listing of such names. (The assistance of Bert Langdon in the preparation of this listing is gratefully acknowledged.)

EDWIN AUGUST	MONTAGUE LAWRENCE
FLORENCE BARKER	PRISCILLA MAY
KATE BRUCE	PHYLLIS FORDE
EDDIE DILLON	CHARLES BERY
GLADYS EGAN	LITTLE GLADYS
ROBERT HARRON	WILLIE McBAIN
DELL HENDERSON	ARTHUR BUCHANAN
GRACE HENDERSON	MARGARET WINTER
JAMES KIRKWOOD	WALTER SCOTT
FLORENCE LA BADIE	GERTRUDE GORDON
MARION LEONARD	LILLIAN BEDFORD

WILFRED LUCAS   ALEXANDER HARVEY
CLAIRE McDOWELL   DORIS CARLTON
FRED MACE   SYDNEY PARKHURST
CHARLES MAILES   HARRY BENSON
CHRISTY MILLER   PERCY HEMMING
CHARLES MURRAY   JAMES O'HARA
MABEL NORMAND   MURIEL FORTESCUE
ALFRED PAGET   GEORGE HARGREAVES
MARY PICKFORD   DOROTHY NICHOLSON
VIVIAN PRESCOTT   VIOLET CRAWFORD
BILLY QUIRK   JAMES WILSON
MACK SENNETT   WALTER TERRY
FORD STERLING   ALBERT WILLIAMS
BLANCHE SWEET   DAPHNE WAYNE
CHARLES WEST   JAMES McCARTHY
HERBERT YOST   BARY O'MORE

Appendix 2
Actresses Who Have Worked for D. W. Griffith

The following list was compiled mainly from *D. W. Griffith*, by Iris Barry and Eileen Bowser (an indispensable source of reference), from Robert M. Henderson's *D. W. Griffith: The Years at Biograph*, and from a personal viewing of the films. ABs here stands for American Biograph pictures.

MARY ALDEN: *The Battle of the Sexes* (1914), *Home Sweet Home, The Birth of a Nation, Intolerance*
LINDA ARVIDSON: ABs
FLORENCE AUER: ABs, *That Royle Girl*
EVELYN BALDWIN: *The Struggle*
FLORENCE BARKER: ABs
VIOLA BARRY: ABs
MRS. MORGAN BELMONT: *Way Down East*
BELLE BENNETT: *The Battle of the Sexes* (1928)
DOROTHY BERNARD: ABs
JOSEPHINE BERNARD: *Way Down East*
EUGENIE BESSERER: *Scarlet Days, The Greatest Question, Drums of Love*

CLARA T. BRACY: ABs

LUCILLE BROWN: *Intolerance*

KATE BRUCE: ABs, *Intolerance, Hearts of the World, A Romance of Happy Valley, The Greatest Thing in Life, The Girl Who Stayed at Home, True Heart Susie, The Greatest Question, The Idol Dancer, Way Down East, Orphans of the Storm, The White Rose, The Struggle*

LILY CAHILL: ABs

JEWEL CARMEN: *Intolerance*

MARIE CHAMBERS: *That Royle Girl*

JOYCE COAD: *Drums of Love*

MIRIAM COOPER: ABs, *Home Sweet Home, The Birth of a Nation, Intolerance*

ROSEMARY COOPER: *Drums of Love*

LUCY COTTON: ABs

JOSEPHINE CROWELL: ABs, *Home Sweet Home, The Birth of a Nation, Intolerance, Hearts of the World, The Greatest Question*

GRACE CUNARD: ABs

MARGARET DALE: *One Exciting Night*

RUTH DARLING: *Intolerance*

DOROTHY DAVENPORT: ABs

ADELE DE GARDE: ABs

CAROL DEMPSTER: *The Girl Who Stayed at Home, True Heart Susie, Scarlet Days, The Love Flower, Way Down East, Dream Street, One Exciting Night, The White Rose, America, Isn't Life Wonderful, Sally of the Sawdust, That Royle Girl, The Sorrows of Satan*

LYA DE PUTTI: *The Sorrows of Satan*

YVETTE DUVOISIN: *Hearts of the World*

GLADYS EGAN: ABs

PEARL ELMORE: *Intolerance*

CATHERINE EMMETT: *Orphans of the Storm*

FLORENCE FAIR: *Sally of the Sawdust*

FLORA FINCH: ABs

EMILY FITZROY: *Way Down East*

EDNA FOSTER: ABs

MARY FOY: *The White Rose*

HELEN FREEMAN: *Abraham Lincoln*

PATRICIA FRUEN: *Way Down East*

DOROTHY GISH: ABs, *Home Sweet Home, Hearts of the World, Orphans of the Storm*

LILLIAN GISH: ABs, *The Battle of the Sexes* (1914), *Home Sweet Home, The Birth of a Nation, Intolerance, Hearts of the World, The Great Love, A Romance of Happy Valley, The Greatest Thing in Life, True Heart Susie, Broken Blossoms, The Greatest Question, Way Down East, Orphans of the Storm*
MARY GISH: *Hearts of the World*
JETTA GOUDAL: *Lady of the Pavements*
OLGA GREY: *The Birth of a Nation, Intolerance*
GRACE GRISWOLD: *One Exciting Night*
ELLA HALL: ABs
KAY HAMMOND: *Abraham Lincoln*
RUTH HANDFORTH: *Intolerance*
MARCIA HARRIS: *Isn't Life Wonderful, The Sorrows of Satan*
MILDRED HARRIS: *Intolerance*
IRMA HARRISON: *One Exciting Night*
JESSIE HARRON: *Hearts of the World*
MRS. HARRON: *Hearts of the World*
PHYLLIS HAVER: *The Battle of the Sexes* (1928)
MARY HAY: *Hearts of the World, Way Down East*
GRACE HENDERSON: ABs
ANITA HENDRY: ABs
EDNA HOGAN: *The Struggle*
FAY HOLDERNESS: *Hearts of the World*
GLORIA HOPE: *The Great Love*
DOROTHY HUGHES: *The Sorrows of Satan*
LURAY HUNTLEY: *Intolerance*
PEACHES JACKSON: *The Greatest Thing in Life*
ZITA JOHANN: *The Struggle*
MARION KERBY: ABs
FLORENCE LA BADIE: ABs
ALICE LAIDLEY: *That Royle Girl*
MRS. DAVID LANDAU: *Way Down East*
LILLIAN LANGDON: *Intolerance*
LUCILLE LA VERNE: *Orphans of the Storm, The White Rose, America, Abraham Lincoln*
FLORENCE LAWRENCE: ABs
ALBERT LEE: *Intolerance*
JENNIE LEE: ABs, *The Birth of a Nation*
MARION LEONARD: ABs
VERA LEWIS: *Intolerance*
STEPHANIE LONGFELLOW: ABs
BESSIE LOVE: *The Birth of a Nation* (?), *Intolerance*

HELEN LOWELL: *Isn't Life Wonderful*
CLAIRE McDOWELL: ABs
HELEN MACK: *The Struggle*
MRS. ARTHUR MACKLEY: *Intolerance*
JEANNIE MacPHERSON: ABs
MAE MARSH: ABs, *The Escape, Home Sweet Home, The Avenging Conscience, The Birth of a Nation, Intolerance, The White Rose*
MARGUERITE MARSH: ABs, *Intolerance*
BESS MEREDYTH: ABs
UNA MERKEL: *Abraham Lincoln*
VIOLET MERSEREAU: ABs
MRS. HERBERT MILES: ABs
MARGARET MOONEY: *Intolerance*
MABEL NORMAND: ABs
LOYOLA O'CONNOR: *Intolerance*
VIVIA OGDEN: *Way Down East*
SALLY O'NEIL: *The Battle of the Sexes* (1928)
SEENA OWEN: *Intolerance*
MARY PHILBIN: *Drums of Love*
MARY PICKFORD: ABs
VIVIAN PRESCOTT: ABs
GERTRUDE ROBINSON: ABs
ALMA RUBENS: *Intolerance*
NELLIE SAVAGE: *The Sorrows of Satan*
CLARINE SEYMOUR: *The Girl Who Stayed at Home, True Heart Susie, Scarlet Days, The Idol Dancer*
EFFIE SHANNON: *Sally of the Sawdust*
FLORENCE SHORT: *The Idol Dancer, The Love Flower, Way Down East*
MARIE SHOTWELL: *Sally of the Sawdust*
PAULINE STARKE: *Intolerance*
MARION SUNSHINE: ABs
BLANCHE SWEET: ABs, *The Escape, Home Sweet Home, The Avenging Conscience*
CONSTANCE TALMADGE: *Intolerance*
KATE TANCRAY: ABs
ROSEMARY THEBY: *The Great Love*
JANE THOMAS: *The White Rose*
FAY TINCHER: *The Battle of the Sexes* (1914), *Home Sweet Home*
LUPE VELEZ: *Lady of the Pavements*

ANNA MAE WALTHALL: *Hearts of the World*
HELEN WARE: *Abraham Lincoln*
IDA WATERMAN: *That Royle Girl*
DOROTHY WEST: ABs
WINIFRED WESTOVER: *Intolerance*
MARGERY WILSON: *Intolerance*
CHARLOTTE WYNTERS: *The Struggle*

Select Bibliography

The following books and magazine articles were the main sources of reference used in the preparation of this volume. The number given against each of these items is used in the text to identify sources.

1. Arvidson, Linda. *When the Movies Were Young.* New York: E. P. Dutton, 1925.

2. Barrett, E. E. "Sweet Gish of Old Drury." *Picturegoer* (London), January 1925.

3. Barry, Iris and Eileen Bowser. *D. W. Griffith.* New York: The Museum of Modern Art, 1965.

4. Bartlett, Randolph. "There Were Two Little Girls Named Mary." *Photoplay* (New York), March 1917.

5. "Before They Were Stars: Miriam Cooper." *The New York Dramatic Mirror* (New York), May 15, 1920.

6. Bodeen, DeWitt. "Blanche Sweet." *Films in Review* (New York), November 1965.

7. ———. "Dorothy Gish." *Films in Review* (New York), August–September 1968.

8. ———. "Lillian Gish: An Appreciation." *The Silent Picture* (London), Autumn 1969.

9. Brownlow, Kevin. *The Parade's Gone By.* New York: Alfred Knopf, 1968. London: Secker and Warburg, 1968.

10. Bruce, Robert. "The Girl on the Cover." *Photoplay* (New York), July 1915.

11. Card, James. "The Films of Mary Pickford." *Image* (Rochester), December 1959.

12. Carr, Harry. "How Griffith Picks His Leading Women." *Photoplay* (New York), December 1918.

13. ———. "The Best-Known, Least-Known Girl." *Motion Picture Magazine* (New York), January 1925.

14. ———. "The Girl Who Is Different." *Motion Picture Magazine* (New York), December 1925.

15. "Clarine Seymour—A Memoir." *Pictures* (London), February 1921.

16. Cushman, Robert B. *Tribute to Mary Pickford.* Washington: American Film Institute, 1970.

17. Dorr, John. "The Movies, Mr. Griffith and Carol Dempster." *Cinema* (Los Angeles), Fall 1971.

18. "Dual Lives." *Photoplay* (New York), September 1920.

19. Dunham, Harold. "Mae Marsh." *Films in Review* (New York), June–July 1958.

20. ———. "Mae Marsh, Robert Harron and D. W. Griffith." *The Silent Picture* (London), Autumn 1969.

21. Everson, William K. "The Films of D. W. Griffith." *Screen Facts* (New York), No. 3.

22. Gassoway, Gordon. "The Wickedest Woman in Pictures." *Picturegoer* (London), April 1921.

23. Gish, Lillian. "D. W. Griffith—A Great American." *Harper's Bazaar* (New York), October 1940.

24. ———. *The Movies, Mr. Griffith and Me.* New York: Prentice-Hall, 1969. London: W. H. Allen, 1969.

25. ———. "Remodelling Her Husband." *The Silent Picture* (London), Spring 1970.

26. Griffith, D. W. "Actresses Must Be Young." *Moving Picture World* (New York), December 27, 1913.

27. ———. "David Wark Griffith Speaks." *New York Dramatic Mirror* (New York), January 14, 1914.

28. "The Griffith Way." *Photoplay* (New York), April 1915.

29. Hall, Gladys. "Why Hollywood Marriages Fail." *Motion Picture Magazine* (New York), February 1930.

30. Hall, Leonard. "An Interview with D. W. Griffith of Biograph." *Stage* (New York), *ca.* 1912.

31. Howe, Herbert. "Hollywood Girls." *Motion Picture Magazine* (New York), June 1922.

32. Lederer, Josie P. "One 'Mae' Day." *Picturegoer* (London), September 1922.

33. Mae Marsh. *Screen Acting.* Los Angeles: Photo-Star Publishing Company, 1922.

34. Naylor, Hazel Simpson. "The Poet-Philosopher of the Photoplay." *Motion Picture Magazine* (New York), September 1919.

35. O'Dell, Paul. "Miriam Cooper: Forgotten Star." *The Silent Picture* (London), Autumn 1969.

36. Owen, K. "The Girl on the Cover." *Photoplay* (New York), April 1915.

37. Paine, Albert Bigelow. *Life and Lillian Gish.* New York: The Macmillan Company, 1932.

38. Pickford, Mary. *Sunshine and Shadow.* London: William Heinemann, 1956.

39. Quirk, James R. "Speaking of Pictures." *Photoplay* (New York), December 1926.

40. "Recollections of a Film Pioneer." *The Screen Writer* (Los Angeles), August 1948.

41. Reed, Dena. "She Tried To Stay Out of the Movies." *The New Movie Magazine* (New York), November 1931.

42. Reid, Laurence. "The Twelve Best Pictures of 1924." *Motion Picture Classic* (New York), January 1925.

43. Robbins, E. M. "The Two Strange Women." *Photoplay* (London), August 1919.

44. Robinson, Selma. "Don't Blame the Movies!" *Motion Picture Magazine* (New York), July 1926.

45. Rochester, Paul. "Lillian Gish: What Love Means to Me." *Picturegoer* (London), October 1924.

46. Rosenberg, Bernard and Harry Silverstein. *The Real Tinsel.* New York: The Macmillan Company, 1970.

47. St. Johns, Adela Rogers. "Black Sheep Gish." *Photoplay* (New York), January 1919.

48. ———. "An Impression of Blanche Sweet." *Photoplay* (New York), September 1924.

49. Scheur, Philip K. "Reminiscing with Lillian Gish." *Los Angeles Times,* December 22, 1968.

50. Shannon, Betty. "An Unfinished Story." *Photoplay* (New York), July 1920.

51. Slide, Anthony. *Lillian Gish.* London: British Film Institute, 1969.

52. Sweet, Blanche. "Griffith, a Big Step Forward and Judith." *The Silent Picture* (London), Winter 1969–70.

53. "A Tale of Two Gishes." *Picturegoer* (London), May 1922.

54. Tozzi, Romano. "Lillian Gish." *Films in Review* (New York), December 1962.

55. Wagenknecht, Edward. *The Movies in the Age of Innocence.* Norman: University of Oklahoma, 1962.

56. Wilcox, Herbert. *Twenty-Five Thousand Sunsets.* London: The Bodley Head, 1967.

57. Wilson, Beatrice. "A Broken Set of Gishes." *Motion Picture Magazine* (New York), April 1929.